COUNTING MY CHICKENS ...

INTRODUCTION BY

TOM STOPPARD

Drawings by Will Topley

Edited by Sophia Topley and Susan Hill

FARRAR, STRAUS AND GIROUX

NEW YORK

COUNTING MY CHICKENS...

And Other Home Thoughts

THE DUCHESS
OF DEVONSHIRE

Farrar, Straus and Giroux
19 Union Square West, New York 10003

Distributed in Canada by Douglas & McIntyre Ltd.
Printed in the United States of America
Originally published in 2001 by Long Barn Books, Great Britain
Published in the United States by Farrar, Straus and Giroux
First American edition, 2002

The pieces in this book, some in different form, originally appeared in
the following publications: the *Daily Telegraph*, the *Telegraph Weekend
Magazine*, the *Sunday Telegraph*, *The Sunday Times*, *County Living*,
Historic House Magazine, *Illustrated London News*, *Woman and Home*,
the *Spectator*, the *British Goat Society Yearbook*, the *Chatsworth Staff
Newsletter*, and *Books and Company*.

Library of Congress Cataloging-in-Publication Data
Devonshire, Deborah Vivien Freeman-Mitford Cavendish, Duchess
of, 1920–
    Counting my chickens . . . and other home thoughts / Deborah
Devonshire ; drawings by Will Topley ; edited by Sophia Topley
and Susan Hill.— 1st ed.
        p.   cm.
    Originally published: Ebrington, Gloucestershire : Long
Barn Books, 2001.
    ISBN 0-374-13029-9 (alk. paper)
    1. Chatsworth (England).   2. Devonshire, Deborah Vivien
Freeman-Mitford Cavendish, Duchess of, 1920–   3. Administration
of estates—England—Chatsworth.   4. Nobility—Great Britain—
Biography.   I. Topley, Sophia.   II. Hill, Susan, 1942–   III. Title.

DA690.C46 D46 2002
942.5'11—dc21
[B]
                                                        2002022812

Designed by Jonathan D. Lippincott

www.fsgbooks.com

1   3   5   7   9   10   8   6   4   2

To

the Co-Editors

with Love

CONTENTS

INTRODUCTION
by Tom Stoppard

Our first house in England was a boy's bicycle ride from Chatsworth, and we went picnicking there in the immediate post-war years, before the house (Chatsworth, that is, not our semi at Calver Sough) was re-opened to the public. My prep school, which seemed so poignantly far from home, and Dovedale, a frequent outing for the family and the pre-war Riley, were close to Chatsworth, too, but I never understood the geography until I returned to Okeover, Dovedale, and Chatsworth some fifty years later as, respectively, a trespasser, tripper, and guest. At the age of eight, I fell in love with England almost at first glance, never considering that the England I loved was, in the first place, only a corner of Derbyshire, and, in the second place, perishable. This book of occasional writings by Deborah Devonshire is not intended as a panegyric, but the overall effect on me is plangent with lament for a lost domain.

The effect, I must add, is achieved, not altogether inadvertently, by stories which made me laugh aloud, and by a general impatience with useless nostalgia or, especially, complaint. Debo's hands are too busy for wringing, her mind too occupied with the present (and the future) to dwell in arrears. And yet the not-so-distant past cannot be kept out of these pages; it backlights the way we live now with our yellow lines, logos, 'consultants,' quires of forms, and all the prescriptions and proscriptions of officialdom that have put the nannies and busybodies in charge; none of which is rued so keenly here as the rift between country life and town, making the one a mystery and an irrelevance to the other. Here in this book, you will find the amazed and disgusted little boy who announced 'I'll never drink milk again' on witnessing the milking demonstration at the Chatsworth Farmyard, and the ecomilitant who rang her neighbour in fury to demand, 'Why have you poisoned the dahlias?' after an unseasonal frost.

It's not funny—or not *only* funny—to Debo, who also knows which puffball fungi are good eating, and about trees, camellias, sheep, goats, chickens, cookery, housekeeping and shopkeeping, and a hundred other things, including pictures and 'the best book on retailing ever written' (*The Tale of Ginger and Pickles*, by Beatrix Potter). Guided by Miss Potter and her own standards, she has made a roaring success of the Chatsworth Farm Shop, whose London outpost in Elizabeth Street, a stone's throw from Victoria Station if you throw towards Belgrave Square, is the only shop I know where you can find Dovedale Blue cheese, not to mention Derbyshire manners, which are almost an anachronism in the metropolis.

There is and can be no sentence in this book which sums its author up, but two of those which stay in my mind are: 'I buy most of my clothes at agricultural shows' and (on receiving a moss tree as a present) 'I pulled it to bits to see how it was made.' So, now you think you've got her? Far from it. She's also mad about Elvis Presley. I've seldom scored such a success with a house present as I did with a signed photo of Elvis.

To be in love with Debo Devonshire is hardly a distinction, and my joining this crowded company occurred in the inaugural year of the Heywood Hill Prize for literature, which is presented at Chatsworth. I was invited by Andrew Devonshire to hand over the cheque and stay the weekend, with the added lure of fishing the Derbyshire Wye at Monsal Dale on the Saturday. At that time of year, dinner and the evening rise happen at much the same time, so one has to miss one or the other, and Debo, mindful of the priorities, excused me from dinner. The company, in best bib, tucker, and jewellery, were at the pudding stage when I tried to sneak past in my Barbour and gum boots. Debo would have none of it. I was sat down next to her, wellies and all, and my dinner, kept warm under a silver dome, appeared in front of me as if by magic. If there was a moment when the mild torture of writing this introduction became irrefusable, that was it.

But is there nothing to be said against our author? Does she disappoint in any department? The slimness of the section titled 'Books and Company' gives a clue. As a literary moll, the Duchess is a hoot. Asked to nominate ten books to take on the Trans-Siberian Railway, she gives up after six, including *Ginger and Pickles*. Her third choice is a book by one of her closest friends, Patrick Leigh Fermor, and a very good book it is, but . . . 'I am sorry to say I have not read it.' Debo explains this by saying she couldn't bear not having it still to read. Later we learn that Evelyn Waugh cannily gave her one of his books with all the pages blank and only the title by which to identify it. But redemption is complete when we read that among the books kept in her bedroom so as not to risk being stolen by guests are *Fowls and Geese and How to Keep Them*, the Quiller-Couch *Oxford English Verse* on India paper, and, 'most precious,' *The Last Train to Memphis: The Rise of Elvis Presley*.

My first recommendation to browsers among the

good stories and useful knowledge herein is 'Road from the Isles,' an account of taking a goat by boat and train in wartime from Mull—no, not from bustling Mull itself, but from an island off the coast of Mull—to London. It's a classic vignette of the Mitford spirit; and it is also, to go out where I came in, a song to old-fashioned self-reliance and a reproach to this era of dependence, when milking the goat between trains in the ladies' first-class waiting room (even though 'I only had a third-class ticket') would bring down five varieties of authority on Debo's golden head. The goat behaved perfectly and was soon pruning sister Nancy's garden in Little Venice. (The story first appeared in the hard-to-find *British Goat Society Yearbook* for 1972, so we must be grateful to Debo's editors for saving it for the rest of us.)

Chatsworth, meanwhile, 'is now more alive than at any time in its history.' Well, we know why.

DIARIES

The first sentence of a diary given to a nine-year-old child at Christmas, written on New Year's Day and kept faithfully till at least 10 January, was 'got up, dressed, had breakfast.' The first sentence of a book is a different matter and very difficult indeed. I have been pondering over this for some time. I asked my sister Jessica what to do. She tells me that in America, if you pay some money, you can get advice as to how to begin and then go on to be a famous author. They say put down 'the' on a bit of paper, add some words, keep on adding, and Bob's your uncle (or the American equivalent), you're off and the rest will follow. It doesn't seem to work. Just try. So, hopelessly stuck and faced with the empty page, see how other people manage. Lately we have been reminded of 'I had a farm in Africa . . .' 'I had a farm in Derbyshire' somehow doesn't sound as good, and anyway it would be a lie, because in England things like farms seldom belong to women. Having failed with 'the,' try 'and.' 'And it came to pass,' too affected, and you can't go on in that biblical style. When you open books to see how it is done, it seems so easy, set down there in the same type as the rest, as if it was no trouble at all, the second sentence flowing out of the first one like one o'clock. Believe me, the writer has suffered over those words. As fifty thousand books are published every year, the first sentences must add hugely to the level of anxiety in an already anxious race.

I looked at the television programme about Uncle Harold,* called *Reputations*. How strange it is to see his and Aunt Dorothy's† private life trotted out like a story in a film. He would have considered the fashion for such entertainment unspeakably vulgar. And so do I. The point about Dorothy Macmillan was her charm, energy, and earthiness; there were no frills. She was one of the few people I have met who was exactly the same with whomever she was talking to, oblivious of

---

*Harold Macmillan.
†Harold's wife, Lady Dorothy, née Cavendish, daughter of the ninth Duke of Devonshire.

their class—something which people keep on about
now almost as much as they do about sex. She gave
her whole attention, laughed easily, was unread and
not smart, and was a tireless constituency worker. I
was always told that it was she who won the elections
at Stockton-on-Tees.* Her time in Downing Street
was famous for children's parties, and the branches,
more than flowers, which she dragged up from the
garden at Birch Grove in the back of her car. When
Uncle Harold was Housing Minister, Andrew, my
husband, was president of the Building Societies' Association. It seemed to be indicated that Andrew
should ask his aunt to the annual dinner as guest of
honour. She asked, 'Shall I wear my best dress or the
other one?' The thought of the other one made us
wonder.

Harold was an intellectual and a politician all
right, no doubt about that; but the mistake so often
made of putting people into categories left him there,
and did not allow for his interest in the family publishing business and many different aspects of life, including his devotion to field sports. The press called
that 'the grouse moor image.' After he married, his

*A predominately industrial constituency in the northeast of En-
gland, which returned a conservative Member of Parliament (Macmillan) against the odds.

father-in-law expected him to go out shooting, even though he had never before fired a shotgun. Reg Roose, a Chatsworth gamekeeper and a delightful man, was detailed to be his tutor. Uncle Harold was a quick learner. Years later, Reg and I watched his performance when large quantities of pheasants flew high across a valley with the wind behind them. 'Doesn't the Prime Minister shoot well?' I said. 'Yes,' answered Reg proudly. 'I taught him and he's fit to go anywhere now.'

When Uncle Harold was ninety, he stayed with us for three months. I will always remember his perfect manners. He dined alone with me often, and I am sure he would have welcomed other company. But he talked as if I were his intellectual equal—ha, ha—or another ex-Prime Minister, and I almost began to think I was. For much of the day, he sat in an armchair in his bedroom and listened to tapes of Trollope. (It made me nervous when he dropped off, lest his smouldering cigar should fall into the wicker wastepaper basket by his side.) He once told me of a mistake made by the suppliers of the tapes. 'I think there is something wrong. They have sent a curious book called *Lucky Jim*, by a feller called Amis. Have you ever heard of him? I don't like it much. Must be a very peculiar man.' He was frail and shuffled down the long corridors at his own speed. He couldn't find the door to the hall, and I heard him mutter, 'The trouble with this house is you have to throw double sixes to get out.'

His relationship with President Kennedy* was worth watching. The President had never seen anything like him, and you could say the same for Uncle Harold. They struck up an unlikely friendship and were more surprised and more amused by each other at every meeting. They talked endlessly on the telephone—usually in the middle of the night. I used to hear of these conversations from both participants. It was the time when initials of organisations began to be used as a sort of shorthand. One night, after speaking of Castro, they went on to discuss SEATO and NATO. Uncle Harold was stumped for a moment when the President said, 'And how's Debo?' When Mrs Thatcher was new to the job he had had for years, she went to see him. 'Oh good,' I said, 'and did you talk?' 'No,' he replied, 'she did.'

Uncle Harold's good manners were often tested when he stayed with us. I am not good at *place à table*, and one night I saw he was sitting at dinner between my son and his friend, both in their first year at Eton. There was the usual political crisis on, and the

*President Kennedy's sister Kathleen married Andrew's brother, Billy Hartington, in 1944.

PM was preoccupied with his own thoughts, while the boys anxiously cast round for a suitable subject of conversation. After a long silence, I heard Sto* say, 'Uncle Harold, *Old Moore's Almanack* says you'll fall in October.' To his eternal credit, after a suitable pause, he answered, 'Yes, I should think that's about right.'

It is strange to see your family enacted on television from an old book about them, written half a century ago. I suppose the royal family and politicians such as Bush and Mandy,† whose ancestors played a part in public life, do so continually. But for ordinary folk, it is indeed an odd experience. It was also odd to read the reviews. Mr Paul Hoggart in *The Times* made me sad. I don't know what wing he favours politically, but his dismal summing-up of what was meant to be high comedy reminded me for all the world of my sister Decca's Communist friends of years gone by. They were incapable of enjoying themselves, had never really laughed at or about anything in their lives, and to

*Nickname of my son Peregrine Cavendish, Marquess of Hartington.
†Peter Mandelson, MP for Hartlepool. His grandfather was Herbert Morrison, created Lord Morrison in 1959, Labour MP and Home Secretary in Winston Churchill's wartime coalition government.

be in their company for long was a lowering experience. Decca saw jokes better than anyone—it was her far-left friends' determination to see the downside of everything that was reminiscent of Mr Hoggart's summing-up of the first episode of *Love in a Cold Climate.** He disapproves in a governessy way of the idea of my father hunting my sisters with his bloodhounds *for fun*. What else would he have done it for? (Alas, I was considered too young to be hunted, and by the time I was of huntable age, the bloodhounds had gone.) I know that some misguided people, for reasons best known to themselves, are against hunting foxes, but surely children are fair game? He complains, too, about a mother's reaction to the hideous appearance of her newborn baby. I wonder if, in his sheltered life, the reviewer has ever seen a newborn baby. Referring to Nancy, he goes on to say that 'she presents her cast as freaks.' Another reviewer states we were the 'lunatic fringe.' Oh dear, freaks and lunatics. Well, never mind.

My sister Nancy's letters have been published,† or some of them I should say, as we have got thousands here. They are kept in cardboard boxes with holes for them to breathe through. Whenever I pass by a pile of

*Based on the 1945 novel by my sister Nancy Mitford.
†*Love from Nancy: The Letters of Nancy Mitford.* Edited by Charlotte Mosley. London: Hodder and Stoughton, 1993.

these boxes, containing papers of every description accumulated since the 1950s, I always hope they are a
consignment of day-old chicks, which used to travel
by train in the guard's van in just such boxes. They
provide what Americans call 'Optimum Archival Conditions.' I don't know about their conditions, but
Nancy's are certainly of Optimum Archival Amuse-
ment. She had neat handwriting and the talent of filling the last page exactly, so 'love from' is always at
the bottom: difficult to achieve if the letter is to make
sense—and hers do. I am not the only one to think she
was the supreme entertainer, both in real life (she and
my father together were better than any turn on the
stage) and on paper. Her letters are just as funny as
her books. What would psychiatrists make of her
teases? She called me 'Nine' because she said that was
my mental age. About right, I expect, but disconcert-
ing when she introduced me to her smart French
friends as 'my little sister aged nine' long after I was
married.

The correspondence has been ably read on the
wireless by Timothy West and Prunella Scales, and listening, I was reminded of Evelyn Waugh's generosity
when he was in Paris just after the liberation. (Why
was he there? Perhaps he was a liberator; I can't remember.) He bought me a hat, which he tried on himself in the shop to make sure. He didn't tell me what
the vendeuse thought about that, but French people

are keen when it comes to business, and a sale is a sale whatever for or why, so no doubt she was delighted and probably thought all English soldiers wore women's hats when off duty. It was made of white felt, with a blue straw brim on which perched two small white stuffed birds. Luckily, the Animal Rights people were still in utero, or Evelyn would have been lynched for buying it and I for wearing it. Sadly, it has gone the way of old hats. Fifty years on, it might be revered as a bit of heritage or a historic document, like a Dinky toy or a 1945 bus ticket. Who knows, it could even have found a home in the V & A with the rest of their jumble.

Nancy's letters often describe clothes. When Dior invented the New Look in 1947, my mother-in-law, 'Moucher' Devonshire, and her friend the Duchess of Rutland, who were in Paris for a less frivolous reason, wanted to see the collection. They arrived at Avenue Montaigne in their tweed overcoats, which had done years of war service, and ditto their shoes. They weren't allowed in. Of humble nature, the two duchesses were disappointed, but not at all surprised. They sat on a bench, eating their sandwiches, to pass the time till they could decently return to the embassy where they were staying.

———

Diana Cooper has died. I admired her beauty and her guts. I was never an intimate friend of hers, but we had many mutual friends, among them Evelyn Waugh and Antony Head.* Both were tickled, for some reasons best known to themselves, because I call my sister Diana 'Honks.' As Cooper was also Diana, they started calling her Honks, too. So the archivists who busy themselves with other people's letters have slipped up several times already and think Evelyn was referring to Diana Mosley (my sister) when it was another old beauty he was on about. Not that it matters much, except it would be hard to find two more different people.

 I have reached the stage in life when I wake up earlier and earlier in the mornings. The wait till breakfast time has forced me to put a kettle and toaster in my room, so I can help myself to their merciful productions whenever I like. I advise all early wakers who have fallen for this plan to buy a clock with a minute

*British politician.

and second hand of immediately recognisable lengths, or you may have my disappointing experience of last week. Waking at 6:00 a.m., I made and ate my breakfast, only to discover that the clock's similar-looking hands had played a trick on me and it was in fact only 12:30 a.m. Too early even for me, but too late to pretend I hadn't had breakfast.

A beautiful new television has been installed. Well, not beautiful, but a big dark object which is dead when turned off and spends a lot of time describing death when turned on.

But it isn't the programmes I'm complaining about; it is the difficulty of making it work. The last one was so nice and simple; you just pushed a sort of matchbox-shaped bit to turn it on and then 1, 2, 3 according to your whim.

It never failed to do as it was told. Now I have had to engage a tutor to coach me in television A levels. I have failed the exam.

There are so many tiny rubbery squares to press on two (why *two*?) handheld, nameless objects that unless you have got long pointed nails (which I have not) and are dead accurate in your aim, you end up with a picture of a rowdy midnight hailstorm instead of racing at Kempton Park or Jon Snow* setting about his victim.

My tutor tells me to pay attention and explains that only four little bits of rubber need be pressed, two on each of the objects, which I clutch in both hands like castanets.

With this vital information ringing in my ears, I go to Bakewell and buy a lot of sticking plasters to cover the unwanted buttons. By this time, I've forgotten which are the right ones and my tutor has gone home.

I shall never know what the other forty are for, and I wish to goodness that the manufacturer would resist putting them there in the first place. Oh, for a telly of yesteryear, just On/Off and channels 1, 2, 3, and 4.

I buy most of my clothes at agricultural shows, and good stout things they are. Much better than the strange-looking garments in desperate colours at one thousand pounds each in the Knightsbridge shops. In the unlikely event of falling for one of those, you will find that all the buttons come off the first time you

---

*Best television newscaster.

wear it, which is disappointing. After agricultural
shows, Marks & Spencer is the place to go shopping,
and then Paris. Nothing in between seems to be much
good. I have learnt to pluck up the courage to go
through the doors of the grand shops in Paris. They
look at you as if you were something the dog brought
home, but once you are inside, the magic of French
talent with clothes takes over and happiness sets in,
until the agonising decision has to be made about
what not to buy, when you long for everything. At
four score years plus, properly made clothes should
last to the end—or that is my excuse. So forgotten
French works of art come out of the back of the cupboard (mixed with Barbours and Derri boots), still
beautiful and always comfortable, which is my idea of
what clothes ought to be.

We all know about old women being knocked down
and having their bags snatched. It has become so ordinary that the newspapers no longer mention it unless
the snatchee is famous and badly hurt, when there are
a few lines at the bottom of the home-news page. In
London, it happens in places like Cadogan Square and
South Audley Street, where I suppose the bag owners

are thought by the snatchers to be rich. I wonder how the victims are chosen. The older the woman, the larger and heavier the bag, but I'm not sure it is always weighed down with diamond necklaces and ruby rings. The contents seem to be stones or coal—or that's what it feels like if you offer to hold it while the owner rearranges her sticks. The snatcher may think he's got a decent reward for his courage in bashing the old soul to the ground, but he must feel let down when he finds only huge bottles of medicines with unpronounceable names. I pity the thief when it's my turn. My bag is positively septic inside, so if he's got any sense, he will wear one of those things that dustmen and dentists cover their noses with when delving into unpleasantness. He will find handfuls of tiresome credit cards sliding about in their meaningless way, heaps of copper coins which don't even buy a newspaper, unanswered letters of top priority, combs in variety, scissors, rubber bands, stamps, an old-age pensioner's railway card, and ballpoints without tops, which all help to make it filthy. If he gets my basket as well, he will rue the day he decided to go in for stealing. It is loaded with iron rations in case of getting stuck on the M1, rock-hard bits of toast meant for the chickens, some Bonham's catalogues, a book I never read but which is another insurance against the mysterious habits of the motorway, the Jacob Sheep Society's (very difficult) quiz in triplicate, plus the minutes of many a tedious meeting. He will be bitterly disappointed with his haul and I will be the reason for at least one thief who decides to go straight.

 While I am on about old women and the awful things that happen to us, there is the ever-present trap of talking to yourself in a loud voice without being aware of it. You are apt to address whatever you are doing, or just speak your thoughts while mechanically getting on with something different, like knitting or making marmalade. A dog can save the day when someone comes round the corner unexpectedly, because it is easy to pretend you were saying something important to Bracken or Nobby. But there are occasions when you have no props and any attempt at explanation would be pointless and would land you deeper in the mire. Last summer, I was walking along a stream in a remote part of our garden. It was at the time of the evening when the people who come round have usually long since gone home. There is a small but deep concrete section of the stream about two feet square, something to do with water from the hill draining into it, I suppose, as the rest of the stream has natural banks and is very shallow. I saw a frog under the wa-

ter in the concreted bit, unable to get up the sheer sides. Thinking it would drown, I plunged my hand into the cold water and picked it out. I thought I'd done a good deed and would get a lifesaving medal from the Frog Preservation Society, when, in the unpredictable way of its kind, it jumped back in. 'Oh, you fool of a frog,' I said very loudly, 'I've never seen such a stupid frog as you. You don't deserve to be saved.' I turned round, and there were two complete strangers who stared at me, obviously thinking that I should not have been let out.

We live in a National Park, and very pleasant it is, too. Planning restrictions are, rightly, fairly rigid, and the planners' deliberations over relatively simple jobs like farm buildings are slow. This is as it should be, and any small irritation is far outweighed by the benefits. Debate over the age-old local industry of quarrying is on at the moment. The winning of minerals from under the ground has gone on in these parts from time immemorial, from the lead mines of yesteryear to the valuable and versatile barytes, fluorspar, and stone quarries of today. The grey-and-green landscape of the lonely limestone High Peak uplands is

netted by drystone walls, making tiny enclosures of
crazy shapes. Every so often, there are sudden deep
clefts in the rocky soil, which form the Derbyshire
Dales, admired and enjoyed by all who know them.
The scenery is more dramatic where the man-made
cliffs of the huge quarries outdo the natural ones, and
just as beautiful in their own stark way. The rules to
do with reinstating worked-out quarries are strict, and
nature sees to it that they soon begin to look like their
natural rocky neighbours as the native flora spreads
itself to clothe the stone faces. Quarrying is now described by the familiar single-issue brigade of protest-
ers as 'a threat to the National Park.' Last week,
a television documentary had a comedian tell us it
ought to be stopped. He wasn't at all funny, and anyway, it is a serious subject. He said, 'Allowing more
quarrying in the Peak Park* is like grinding up York
Minster for motorway hardcore.' I wonder what material he thinks York Minster is built of and where it
came from. No quarry, no Minster. He went on, 'The
Peak District is a far cry from the paradise envisaged
by the people who set up the parks.' I suppose he
thinks that putting people out of work makes a paradise. Now schoolchildren are being indoctrinated

*The Peak District National Park, created in 1951, was the first in
England. It covers 556 square miles.

against the industry. A friend of mine who is a county councillor in another part of the country received letters from a class of ten-year-olds with an identical message, obviously dictated by their teacher. They complained of birds and bees being frightened away by work in a local quarry. My friend wrote back, 'Are you driven to school along a road? Do you live in a house? Has it occurred to you that roads and houses are made of stone and that stone comes out of quarries?' If the television comedian and the teacher have their way, we shall soon be importing aggregate for roads and stone for building in spite of sitting on millions of tons of the stuff. Can you imagine anything madder?

The complainers complain about everything. They don't like foxhounds, crowing cockerels, or quarrying, and now they say car-boot sales must be stopped. I suppose we are to be denied the chance of buying a Constable in a muddy field and taking it to the *Antiques Roadshow* so Henry Wyndham* can tell us we have bought a fortune for two pounds. Oh dear. Long live banned work and play.

---

*Sotheby's Chairman Europe and picture expert. Since 1986, he has appeared regularly as a valuation specialist on the television programme the *Antiques Roadshow*.

Most people in this country must have whirled along roads and past fields enclosed by stone walls. Few stop to think how (or when) they were built or to consider the skill of the people who built them.

This week, the annual competition held by the Derbyshire branch of the Dry Stone Walling Association was held on a windy hill high up in the Peak District.

I took the chairman of one of the most respected antique shops in London to see how the experts do it. Not surprisingly, he had never seen such a thing before.

'To be a good waller,' the master craftsman told us, 'you must have eyes and hands which act together: an eye for a stone of the right size and shape for its place and hands which feel the balance instinctively as soon as you pick it up. You can only teach so much; the rest is in you. You've either got it or you haven't.'

The construction of a wall is a building lesson in miniature, from the placing of the big foundation stones to the 'battered'—or tapered—sides and the coping stones laid along the top. There is no mortar or other binding agent to hold them together.

They depend on the 'throughs,' stones long enough to reach right through the wall, holding the sides together and acting as ties to prevent bulging. As the sides are built up, small stones, or fillings, are packed in the middle to prevent them from collapsing inwards. A well-built wall stands for many years, containing the farm stock and providing shelter from gales, rain, and snow for outwintered ewes and lambs.

The membership of the DSWA is made up of full-time professional wallers and an increasing number of men and women who earn their living in totally different ways, from insurance broking to dentistry. These people go walling for the satisfaction of mastering another difficult skill, in contrast to their usual work. 'It is a wonderful relaxation. I get completely lost in it,' a doctor said.

Late in the afternoon, we looked at the finished lengths of what seemed impeccable work to my amateur eye, apparently identical in excellence. The expert on eighteenth-century furniture studied the twentieth-century walling and made his own judgement. 'First, second, third,' he said to me, pointing to his choices. When the real judge added up the points and announced the winners, his placings were in the same order.

The point of this saga is that if your eye is experienced in recognising quality in one form of art, it is often able to do so in another. And surely drystone walling is an art.

Two foods which are prime examples of the capricious ways of Mother Nature are wild mushrooms, which taste so different from the tame kind, and grouse, which don't have a tame kind. They are both a conjuring trick—now you see them, now you don't. You can't make plans for them, because they make their own rules. In one season, there can be plenty of grouse on one moor and pitifully few on another a few miles away, where the conditions in winter and spring—often blamed for a poor hatching and rearing time—have been identical. It is the same with mushrooms. We are told if fertiliser is put on a grass field, or if it is ploughed and re-seeded, there will be no mushrooms. Neither is true, but a mushroom field which is good one year and receives no different treatment the next can be barren. Why? We want rain for mushrooms, they say. The rain comes, but the mushrooms don't. Then when they do appear, they are so full of maggots that they are inedible. But when everything goes right, they are food for the gods.

The unexplained ups and downs of the grouse population are part of their fascination for anyone who is interested in what is now called 'wildlife.' Salmon used to have the same mystique, but now they are 'farmed' and found in every restaurant in the country—cheaper than cod, they have lost the mystery of Williamson's Salar.* But grouse are still truly wild and no attempt to 'farm' them has been successful. Even the gamekeepers, whose lives are spent on the moors, cannot always explain the swing in the numbers of grouse: from feast to famine and back to feast. The graph looks like a cardiogram of a desperately ill heart patient. After a record year, when too many birds are left on the ground, disease strikes and few survive. Such is their power of recovery that they can increase in number again in next to no time. I am glad that the ways of grouse and mushrooms remain unexplained. There are lots of books on mushrooms (but few on grouse) and the vast number of fungi we used to lump together and call toadstools. Experts arrange forays which you can join to learn about which kinds are edible and which will do you in immediately. Look out—the differences are not always as obvious as you might think.

---

*Henry Williamson (1895–1977) was one of the first authors to romanticise species of wildlife. His books include *Tarka the Otter* (1927) and *Salar the Salmon* (1935).

A new treat for us is puffballs—the bigger the better—super-delicious when sliced and fried. Luckily, few English people fancy them. In the same way that our fishermen throw away pike, puffballs are kicked to bits by disappointed mushroomers—to the dismay of any Frenchman, for whom both are a delicacy. When you are tired of blackberrying and get bolder in the search for free food, try 'Chicken of the Woods.' They are those whitish growths on the bole of an oak which look like enormous plates. You will have to carry a heavy and offensive weapon to dislodge them from their host, but it is worth the trouble when they are cooked and you discover not only a new taste but a new consistency.

Our kitchen is being repainted and retiled, so a great clearing of decks is going on. We found a box of menu cards dating from 1893 to 1939 behind a wall of receipt books in the back of a cupboard. They are printed or handwritten on stiff white card with gilt edges. Buckingham Palace, Derby House, Seaford House, Londonderry House, Devonshire House, the King's Guard St James's Palace, the Foreign Office, and the Astors at

4 St James's Square evidently fed their guests very well. Some cards are tantalisingly anonymous, giving only the address. Who lived at 66 Brook Street in 1939? She gave a lavish ball supper there on 25 June. And the unknown occupier of 38 Bryanston Square* did even better a month earlier. We know the vast number of courses people ate at grand dinners in Edwardian times, but it is surprising to find such feasts were still going strong till the last war. If you had been invited to Mr Baldwin's farewell dinner at 10 Downing Street on 25 May 1937, you would have eaten *Consommé à la Sévigné*, *Filets de Soles Impériale*, *Noisettes d'Agneau Châtelaine*, *Petits Pois*, *Pommes nouvelles*, *Cailles sous la Cendre*, *Salade de Laitues*, *Asperges vertes*, *Sauce Mousseline*, *Mousse glacé aux Fraises*, *Frivolités*, *Dessert*, *and Café*, plus five superb wines, ending with Grand Fins Bois 1820. The indiscretions induced by so many fine wines would make any prime minister shudder now. And I don't think they would dare offer *frivolités* today. The humble grapefruit was a luxury then. Several dinners started with them—the only English word on the menus except eggs and bacon, for which there is no satisfactory translation into French. They were fried up for breakfast at 1:45 a.m. at every ball.

---

*The occupant of 38 Bryanston Square was South African magnate Sir Abe Bailey.

At an afternoon reception given by His Majesty's Government in the United Kingdom of Great Britain and Northern Ireland for Commanding General Sir Kaiser Shumshere Jung Bahadur Rana KBE of Nepal, in 1937, the selection of teatime food is a child's dream, or a grown-up's, for that matter. The guests were offered ices, cakes, éclairs, five kinds of sandwiches including foie gras, lobster and caviar, *petits pains fourrés*, wine cup, and every non-alcoholic drink imaginable, including *thé*. I would love to know if Sir Kaiser went on to face a seven-course dinner at 8:30, followed by an immense supper at midnight.

A surprisingly extravagant entertainment was a *souper de bal* given by the Framework Knitters' Company at Goldsmiths' Hall in 1937. That night, you could choose from twenty dishes, including consommé, chicken, cutlets, salmon, lobster, foie gras, quail, duck, *chaud-froid* of more chicken, ham, tongue, asparagus, salad, compote of fruit, crème brûlée, chocolate mousse, and meringues. This was supper. You had already eaten dinner. Lastly comes a refreshing reminder of Evelyn, Duchess of Devonshire's careful ways. The menu for luncheon after the wedding of her son Charlie Cavendish and Adele Astaire (Fred's sister) at Chatsworth in 1932 lists several dishes, including French pastries and two more puddings, crossed out. 'Need not have these' is in her handwriting. The Framework Knitters were not so economical.

The roof is forever being mended, one and a half acres of it. Last week, the men found a copy of the *Manchester Guardian* dated 29 May 1877 under the old lead. The names of all who had worked on the roof then were recorded in the margin in thick pencil. Interesting, but not unusual here. And the headline on the 116-year-old newspaper seemed familiar: AUSTRIA & THE BOSNIAN INSURGENTS. SERBIA PREPARING FOR WAR. SPECIAL TELEGRAM FROM OUR RAGUSA CORRESPONDENT. There followed a description of atrocities . . .

Windows. We have got to have them to keep out weather and burglars. As they are part of the architectural scheme of things, like walls and doors, their make and shape has changed over the centuries with fashion.

In the nineteenth century, newly invented plate glass was greeted with joy, but it made the houses look pitifully blind from the outside. Now we have something worse: plate glass with a narrow slit above, the only part which opens. Any chance of pleasing proportion goes west and the afflicted house is like one partially sighted, with a frightful wink.

The next-door neighbour goes in for a thin brown lattice. How, or if, this kind of window opens and shuts, I don't know, but I do know that these disfigurements have spread like a contagious disease through our towns and villages and are more than a minor tragedy.

They are everywhere, degrading the appearance of perfectly good buildings, whether built of stone or brick. There is no regard for the vernacular because they are just shoved in, new and uniform, from Glasgow to Glastonbury.

Now here's your chance, Mr Minister of Education. In your next curriculum, do beg your teachers to add decent fenestration lessons to the indecent sex lessons so popular with the children. Not as exciting, I suppose, but windows last longer than sex, whatever way you look at it.

If you fail, we must all go out and live in the sultan's palace in Zanzibar, where there isn't any glass to vex the eye and the birds, bats, and bees fly in and out of the rooms on the balmy air of the island of cloves.

I am fascinated by watching and listening to keen gardeners going round other people's gardens. Something strange seems to seize otherwise normal folk and, although they have probably travelled miles for their treat, they show themselves to be really interested only in what they have left at home. People who haven't got gardens of their own can stand back and delight in the big picture of someone else's work, but the real gardener fastens on some small plant, pleased if it doesn't look too well and triumphant if it is dead. They relate the plants to their own. 'Oh, we've got that, but ours is much bigger. I think this one is planted on the wrong wall; it can't stand east. Well, wouldn't you think they'd know that?' When the boot is on the other foot and you are taken by the owner on a two-hour tour in foul weather, it can be difficult to keep up a continuous flow of admiration. Sometimes, before setting out, you are sized up by the hostess to see if you are worth it, and it is rather wonderful when she decides you aren't. That is why it is such a luxury to be able to go round so many gardens in your own time by paying at the door. You can dwell over what you love and hurry by the kidney-shaped beds with raised concrete edges full of orange rhododendrons. My father-in-law (who understood plants) said people go through five stages of gardening. They begin by liking flowers, progress to flowering shrubs, then autumn foliage and berries; next they go for leaves, and finally the underneaths of leaves. Alpines ought to come in somewhere. They can become an addiction, and they get smaller and smaller relative to their importance. In the Wisley collection,* there is a weeny blob of grey leaves among small stones of the same colour. In the spring, a label with an arrow says PLEASE NOTICE FLOWER. Charles de Noailles, a celebrated French gardener, ended by preferring labels to flowers, foliage, or even alpines. I think the attendants of the stalls of the magic displays at the Horticultural Society's shows in the Vincent Square halls are the most patient of beings. Just listen to some old trout describing to her trapped victim what has happened to her *Desfontainia spinosa hookeri* and you will realise that the stall holder is taking the place of a psychiatrist for a free consultation while all is unburdened and the *Desfontainia* lady gets rid of her feelings.

Gardening is almost too difficult to contemplate, but arranging flowers is impossible. I wonder if the arrangers get cross because their work doesn't last. My mother's explanation for the uncertain tempers of cooks was the inevitable destruction of their art thrice daily being enough to unhinge their minds. If the flower people don't get cross, they must be sad when the products of hours of work end in the dustbin. It

*The educational and show garden of the Royal Horticultural Society in Surrey.

has all become too complicated. There are rules, and criticism is fierce. I marvel at the skill which goes into the feats you find in hotels, at wedding receptions, and at flower festivals in churches, but I do not wish to see them in my own house. Everything is too contrived and clever; the flowers spring out of squashy green stuff instead of a good old vase or pot. Since the invention of plastic flowerpots, it is a joy to see one made of proper earthenware, but I expect it would lose points in a floral art competition. The whole subject needs simplifying and straightening as well. Those sideways stalks are worrying and against nature, but then, nature hasn't got much to do with it. I think the Americans are miles ahead in the art. In a long life, during which I have had the luck to be surrounded by beauty, I have never seen anything better than the flowers on the tables at the grand dinner given for the lenders to the 'Treasure Houses of Great Britain' exhibition in Washington. About two hundred diners sat at round tables of eight in a vast hall which goes up the whole height of the National Gallery. Some genius put tall, narrow vases with equally tall flowers on plinths high above the heads of the diners so they could see the people opposite without interference. The result was stunning. Had I done them, I should have had no better idea than a dreary plate with a few blooms floating about in it.

I wish gardening wasn't so difficult. It is almost impossible to look with pleasure or interest at the lists of wallflower seeds to be planted now for next year when this year's are beginning to go over and look as depressing as only dying flowers can. You must steel yourself to do it if you want wallflowers next year.

Another problem is the bewildering choice. Open the catalogue at delphiniums, for instance, and you find page after page of descriptions so glamorous, you want them all and need the concentration of Einstein to reduce the list to something reasonable.

Then you must wait till the year after next to see the fruits of your labour. As likely as not, the supplier has sent the very ones you didn't choose, but you will long since have lost the carefully marked catalogue, so there is nothing to be done.

It is the same with roses. They all sound irresistible, and you must pinch yourself in midwinter, when they are dormant, to remember how monstrously ugly the man-made orange ones are, retina irritants to a rose.

I prefer vegetables, but still there is the difficulty of choice. Pin down the best pea or bean, remember to plant a few every fortnight to avoid feast or famine, and you are indeed a real gardener.

Someone has had a jolly time thinking up names. Even the professors who have so kindly written to me to tell me what a quantum leap is may be stumped by Howard's Lancer, Black Velvet, Captivator, Leveller, and Whinham's Industry, gooseberries all.

The National Rhubarb Collection, believe it or not, contains more than one hundred varieties. I won't weary you with all their names, but you might fancy Grooveless Crimson. I don't think Early White Stone is an advertising man's dream description of a turnip, but whoever christened the parsnip Tender and True was a poet of the kitchen garden.

The oddest of all is the radish called French Breakfast. I have never seen a Frenchman tucking in to radishes for his *petit déjeuner*, but that is what they would have you believe.

The prettiest flowers I have ever seen in a small dining room were in a New York flat: lilies of the valley bolt upright in twos and threes in a bed of moss all down the middle of the table. The best at a dance were white foxgloves, one at a time in proper flowerpots, round the floor of a sitting-out room. Trying to do as well myself, I bought some china vases made like old Crown Derby crocus pots, with holes in the lids to stick the flowers in. Delighted to have found something which forced the stalks to stand up straight, I showed them to a floral art friend, who said, 'What, ten little soldiers?' Yes, ten little soldiers are just the thing. One Easter in our Devonshire Arms Hotel at Bolton Abbey, I had what I thought was a good idea: birds' nests on the restaurant tables with marzipan eggs. So I asked the dried-flower ladies if they could make birds' nests, and along came some good tries. They looked really nice till the customers ate the eggs. As a robbed nest is the saddest sight going and looks like a cowpat with a rim, the manager soon banished them.

Moss is the thing. I have been given (by Americans, needless to say) a moss tree, extremely pretty and more or less everlasting, I'm told, unless you put it in the sun, where it will fade. I pulled it to bits to see how it was made. It is a ball of moss about eighteen inches in diameter, mounted on chicken wire and stuck into place with huge hairpins. It is supported by

a stem of birch held in a basket filled with plaster—
the base of the 'tree' is covered in moss of a different
kind, to hide it. The librarian at Chatsworth happens
to know all about moss; he is no less than the trea-
surer of the British Bryological Society. Seeing this
beauty, he said without hesitation, 'Oh, that's *Leuco-
bryum glaucum*, it only grows in the south of England.' So I see myself taking a van to some distant
damp spot like West Sussex to get the precious raw
material. I expect moss gathering is against the law,
like picking primroses, and I shall have my head cut
off; but if any of us here can succeed in making such a
decorative object, it will be worth it.

At this time of year, I am struck by the racist ways of
that mild section of our fellow countrymen—people
who feed the birds. They go to great lengths to ensure
that only the charming little birds, preferably prettily
coloured and able to sing later on, get the delicacies
provided. The 'country' magazines carry advertise-
ments of complicated arrangements which keep out
the big ugly floppy ones, or any species the bird table*

*A bird table is one on which bird food is spread—not a birdbath.

owner doesn't fancy. Yet these same people are mad
on raptors of all kinds, and even the murderous mag-
pie, but at conveniently far remove. It would be interesting to see their reactions if a sparrow hawk or a
merlin chose to swoop while they happened to be
watching and the loved tits, robins, and chaffinches
were reduced to a flurry of feathers in a split second.
If they saw a pair of magpies hunting a hedge for eggs
and nestlings in the spring, they would surely be sick-
ened by the sight of the desperate attempts of the par-
ent birds to distract their attention. But people don't
see the balance of nature acted out beak and claw, so
they follow the fashion, which is to preserve all birds
of prey, whatever the cost to the rest. Unless there is a
change of heart soon, the bird tables will no longer
provide the pleasure that once they did.

Last week, I went into the garden to look at something the hot weather had brought out. While I was
staring at it and thinking of nothing in particular,
there was a rush of wings and a vicious sparrow hawk
dived from nowhere and caught a blue tit, which let
out a small bird's version of a scream. The hawk, usually so precise in its fatal sweep, somehow entangled
itself between a rose hedge and a yew hedge where my
ancient spaniel was happily mousing. His reaction
was to grab the hawk, thinking, I suppose, that it was
that bird of very little brain, a pheasant. I nearly got

to them, but, alas, the old dog realized his mistake after a vicious nip from the hooked beak, and the hawk extricated itself. It flew away to catch and *pluck while still alive* its daily ration of three songbirds, plus a racing pigeon or two, so precious to their owners. Parliament has decreed that these hateful creatures are 'protected.' If the spaniel had hung on, would he have been sent to prison for killing it? I must ask our policeman. It never ceases to surprise me that the same people who enjoy watching the violent and often revolting wildlife films of birds and animals disembowelling one another on the telly are against fox hunting and for hawks and the other disembowellers. The Great British Public is very contrary. So are our legislators.

The pullets arrived early this year. The old hens were moved into one house to make room for the young ones, so smart and neat to look at. All were shut in for two days to make sure they went back to the proper house at night. In spite of this time-honoured way of explaining to chickens where home is, several of the old girls

went back to their original houses, only to find the pullets installed. They were not pleased. They looked as puzzled as you and I would be if we returned to our bedroom to find it crammed full of strange teenagers. Some of these teenagers have started laying very small eggs of superb quality, which are not appreciated by housewives, as they are a far cry from the big eggs we are told we must eat. To explain their lack of size, we put a notice in the Farm Shop saying: 'Pullets' eggs, half price,' but this means nothing, because few know what a pullet is. Oh dear!

If second childhood means going back to first loves in old age, then I am deep in it. As children, my sisters and I kept poultry and sold the eggs for pocket money. Now I have pens of Light Sussex and Welsummers in the garden at Chatsworth, and the pleasure I get from them is enormous.

In middle age, when looking after my own chickens was too complicated, I gathered together pottery and china hens and ducks. They are less trouble than the live kind and are ever-present in my bedroom and sitting room. My favourites are a Belgian faïence pair of life-sized speckled hens with heads turned back and beaks buried in their feathers, in that expression of poultry contentment hens wear after a dust bath on a spring day. One has a brood of chicks poking out from her breast, the other an egg. They are dishes—the top halves lids, heads and necks the handles.

I bought them from one of those expensive antique shops that catered for rich tourists in Park Lane, long since replaced by a travel agency. I remember stopping and staring at them with a great longing. The price seemed wild at the time, and it certainly was. A recent valuation put the dishes at less than I paid twenty years ago, but the price is not the point when one is grabbed by such a longing. They have given, and continue to give, great pleasure.

A pottery nest with chicks hatching and hatched from jagged broken eggshells is also well loved. I have never seen another such group and would love to know where it was made. One chick has only its head out of the egg, another has a bit of shell stuck on its behind, and the third is fully hatched, wearing the surprised look of a chick that's found itself, dry and facing an uncertain world.

I have fallen for paintings of hens, too. An enormous canvas of double-combed Derbyshire Redcaps by T. Benson hangs in my bedroom in our house at Bolton Abbey. William Huggins, taking time off from painting lions, is the artist responsible for another group of poultry, in which the iridescent green-and-black tail feathers of the cock are brilliantly painted. In Théophile-Alexandre Steinlen's lithograph of a cock and two hens (called a trio in the trade, the eternal triangle in this case), you can see from their expressions that he is portraying a prosperous gentleman, his dowdy wife in black feathers, and his flighty mistress—all on one perch.

The behaviour of poultry is like human behaviour and it is just as predictable. They fight; they resent newcomers; they hate wind and rain. Some are bold and forage far from home and some hardly bother to go out-of-doors. They practice a bit of racial argy-bargy, and their purposeful walk when hurrying into the house to lay is like that of determined women heading for the sales. They queue to use the same nesting box (why, when there is a row of identical boxes?), and when they haven't got time to queue, they climb on top of the first comer, to her intense annoyance. Some are neat in appearance and habit, but the Isa Browns are sloppy and have no idea of chic. They seem to be permanently losing a feather or two, instead of having a good moult, getting it over, and then looking smart again, bright of eye and comb. These feckless females drop their eggs anywhere on the floor of their house or on the ground outside. Our long-suffering guests are subjected to collecting the eggs, the high spot of my day. They pretend to enjoy it, but I notice a careful examination of the soles of London shoes when we get home.

I can't remember laughing out loud at anything I have read in *The Times* for years till a piece from the Washington correspondent about American nannies appeared. I thought the point of Americans was that they don't have nannies, that women are judges and all sorts of other things, while the children bring themselves up. A notable example of the system, I thought, was Mark Thatcher's* half-American baby, whose legs, still at the pipe-cleaner stage, were shoved into navy blue dungarees at a month old, obviously expected to go out to work pronto. Just to complicate the issue, a woman called Ms Ireland, who is leader of the women's organisation called the National Organization for Women, is on the prowl to discredit men who have important jobs in Clinton's administration. These despicable fellows may have employed women

*Mark Thatcher is the son of former Prime Minister Margaret Thatcher.

to look after their children. What I'd like to ask Ms Ireland is, How did these men get their children in the first place? Could it be that yet another woman was involved? Not Ms Ireland, of course. Perish the thought that she could have been in close enough contact with a man to result in a baby, who might even demand some years of luxury in the lap of an illegal nanny. Excitement mounts daily. Now we find that Ms Ireland might have bitten off more than even she can chew. Arising out of pretty Judge Kimba Wood's five-day training course as a Bunny, Ms Ireland is to discover how many men in the administration read *Playboy* magazine, or, horror of horrors, went to a Playboy Club. At the tribunals, dear, sweet Ms Ireland will stump onto a rostrum and force the poor little men with important jobs to bow their heads and plead guilty to these crimes as well as getting the housework done for them while they live it up in the law courts. I trust she won't come here. She would find things which would make her hair stand on end.

I have been in America and enjoyed myself enormously, but I find the language is getting difficult. An advertisement in the *Wall Street Journal* reads: 'Need a hand when figuring out where to open a Roth IRA?' I certainly would, and I bet you would, too. Advertising an expensive raffle: 'See Jackie O's necklace in person at the following locations . . .' President Clinton's little local difficulty had just hit the press and produced some memorable stuff: 'Miss Lewinsky lied and lied again and thought her credibility was being questioned.' Ms Goldberg, Linda Tripp's literary agent, was quoted as saying: 'I told her to sleep on it. This is not something that ladies do, to tape each other.' I agree with Ms Goldberg, but I know I'm old-fashioned.

The purpose of my visit was to give some talks. I boldly spoke on Hardwick Hall* to a delightful audience in Los Angeles, who politely listened to the story of that extraordinary house. Afterwards, I met some of the audience to answer their questions. One asked if there are facilities at Hardwick Hall. Not sure what she meant, I said, 'No,' in case she arrived in the summer hoping for massage, pools, and hairdresser. Many were keen students of books written by my sisters Nancy and Jessica and wished to know more about

---

*Fine Elizabethan house built by Bess of Hardwick and architect Robert Smythson between 1591 and 1597. The property came into the Cavendish family through Bess's marriage to Sir William Cavendish and was taken by the government as part payment of death duties following the death of the tenth Duke of Devonshire in 1950.

the Hons Cupboard.* A sad-looking lady asked me if I had been denied education. 'Afraid so,' I said.

No one told me how pretty the country is around Los Angeles. The steep valleys and immaculate gardens are very attractive, but you never see anyone about. I wondered about the right to roam and if one could go for a walk through the prickly scrub on the hillsides. No one knew. Perhaps no one has tried. I was dumbfounded by the two-hundred-acre garden at the Huntington Library. Closely planted cactuses from the desert are within shouting distance of a valley thick with camellias as shiny-leaved as those which grow in the mists of Ireland. How is that done? In Pasadena, there is an English tearoom run by expatriates, called Rose Tree Cottage. So popular is it that you must book for the twice-daily teas, where you sit surrounded by Derby china, Marmite, marmalade, and pictures of Windsor Castle. What impressed me most about the new Getty Museum was not so much the building, its situation, or the wonders to be seen there, but the unforgettable sight of John Walsh, the director, holding open a swinging door for ages while a torrent of people of all shapes, sizes, and colours

---

*The linen cupboard, the warmest place in our house, where we met as children to escape the grown-ups. *Hon* meant 'hen' in Honnish, our secret language.

poured through, ignorant of his identity. He must be the reason for the wonderful atmosphere which hits you as soon as you enter the tram to go up the mountain. It is all the more surprising for a brand-new building. Other museum directors, please note.

Beware the difference in pronunciation of English and American. It changes the meaning of words which are spelt the same, so you have to pay attention when listening to someone from the New World and translate as you go. I met a Texan woman the other day who spoke at length about one Korda. I thought she must be too young to have known Sir Alexander of that ilk; then I suddenly twigged it was President Carter she was on about. 'Gonna' meaning 'going to' and 'wanna' for 'wanting to' are easy, but watch out for riders when they are talking about writers and be prepared for a waiter to turn into a wader without warning. So writers ride and waiters wade, which isn't surprising when a dot is a dart and a pot is a part. It happens here, too. Last night, I heard someone describe the predicament of buttered wives.

———

The two best days of entertainment of the year took place here last weekend: the Fifteenth Country Fair. It was enjoyed by fifty thousand people, watching or taking part in every conceivable country sport, skill, or pastime, from clay shooting, fly casting, catapults, falconry, archery, stunt aeroplanes—too frightening to watch—terrier racing, and gun-dog displays. Jemima Parry-Jones brought her birds of prey. On a still day, one of her peregrines rose higher and higher, till it was a speck in the sky. Jemima swung a lure of raw meat on a string round and round and the bird made a spectacular swoop, its wings folded so that it dived like an arrow at one hundred miles an hour. The stars of the show were the King's Troop, which bring a lump to the throat when they gallop into the ring, pulling their heavy gun carriages and making the earth tremble. They perform an intricate dance, harnesses jangling and wheels missing one another by inches, at a furious pace, till they thunder out of the ring still at the gallop. Mr Blobby marches with any band he can latch on to, followed like the Pied Piper by a crowd of children. The rows of shops here are nearer home than Bond Street, the assistants are much more pleasant, and a wardrobe against the Derbyshire winter was bought in no time. The music of the pipe bands goes through the head for days after the event. Desert

Orchid* was cheered, and the ferret racing drew its own crowd of fans. The best notice was a sign saying LURCHERS' CAR PARK. I don't know how many lurchers can read, let alone drive, but it looked pretty full, and the occupants piled out of their cars and raced against one another all day.

It may be the silly season in London, but it is a serious time of year in Derbyshire. The opera festival in Buxton has been in full swing, the bed-and-breakfasts are bunged up with people enjoying the evenings in the beautifully restored Matcham Opera House of 1903 and the days wandering in the town, buying picnics at Mr Pugson's cheese and delicatessen shop.

I hope they are shocked by the state of Carr of York's magnificent Crescent† of 1780, now boarded up and desolate, awaiting rescue by local government. They can see the source of Buxton water bubbling up, surprisingly, in a room off the Tourist Information Centre.

*Outstanding and much-loved grey steeplechaser, who, since his retirement from racing in 1991, makes popular celebrity appearances.
†A Georgian building in Buxton enclosing thermal baths, built for William Cavendish, fifth Duke of Devonshire, by John Carr of York.

They will be delighted by the dome of the Devon-shire Royal Hospital, bigger than that of St Peter's in Rome. This extraordinary building was the stable for the horses belonging to visitors taking the waters, and the old covered ride for exercising them in bad weather is now the place for practising wheelchairs.

The High Sheriff's cocktail party, with its reassur-ing parade of mayors and their shiny cars, is over. So is Bakewell Show. This annual ritual draws a big crowd even in a temperature of 37°C, this year's scorcher.

The summer national dress of English country-women—cotton skirts, anorak, and gum boots—was the rule as the wind whipped us into the tents.

Poultry and rabbits, with their devoted followers in as much variety as the exhibits, was a good place to escape the weather. I thought I knew poultry, but I was stumped by the breed names of one class—Fur-nace, Polecat, and Salmon Blue. I bet you don't know they are types of Old English game birds.

Most of the egg classes were won by a reverend and his son. I like to think of those two in their vic-arage garden, looking after pens of Marans, Welsum-mers, and other layers of mahogany brown eggs, which produced the perfectly matched winning en-tries.

The floral art exhibitors must be devils for punishment and have a strong streak of masochism to be able to bear the judges' biting criticism. However hard they try, there is something wrong with the strange edifices of whichever material is ordained by the show schedule, topped by a flower and a leaf or two.

I would give up after spending hours trying to shove a lily and a fern into yards of velvet, bits of glass, or a straw teddy bear, only to find the judge's note saying: 'A good attempt, but you should try to be flatter in front' or 'A pity there is a crease in your base.' Difficult for some lady competitors to obey the first directive and impossible for anyone to comply with the second.

 Earlier this week, I drove through the higher reaches of beautiful Wharfedale to give a talk to a Women's Institute. I was reminded (not that I needed reminding, as I live among such people, thank God) of the quality of the silent majority who live out their lives without bothering the headlines and are the backbone of our country.

The WI allows no nonsense like letting men in. It is the female reply to White's, and the other London clubs which stand firm against admitting women members. So that's good.

But I hear there is a move to get away from the 'Jam and "Jerusalem"' image. If so, they make a great mistake and will miss the nostalgia bus which gathers speed daily. The homemade-food stall at any money-raising event is cleaned out in a few minutes.

It is what people love, so why should the WI *wish* to get away from that at which they excel? Jam is the thing and long may it remain so. As for 'Jerusalem,' we sing it almost without thinking about the words. The idea of WI members being brought a bow of burning gold, a spear, and a chariot of fire and their swords not sleeping in their hands fills me with terror. Even Genghis Khan would retreat in the face of this lot.

 Our nearest big town is Chesterfield, and a very good place it is. A few years ago, the sign announcing that you had arrived there read CHESTERFIELD—CENTRE OF INDUSTRIAL ENGLAND. It has been changed to CHESTERFIELD—HISTORIC MARKET TOWN. Why? I suppose industry is out of fashion.

We have just come back from the Republic of Ireland, staying at Lismore Castle, a house we know well, this being the forty-seventh year we have spent part of April there.

Of course, there have been vast changes after so long, but some things are reassuringly the same and happen to time, as they did half a century ago.

The great-great-great and more grandchick of the 1947 heron arrives to fish at the same spot at the same time on the riverbank under the sitting room.

A familiar draught comes through the same gap where the door has never shut properly, the cow parsley and chestnut trees come into flower on the usual date, whatever the weather, the wood anemone come up blue under the oaks, and there are still red squirrels in the tallest yews I know.

The slow coming of the Irish spring is as pleasant as ever, starting earlier and going on longer than that of its neighbouring island to the east. The temperate climate keeps winter and summer pretty well alike.

Touring friends coming from the west coast report huge improvements to hotels and restaurants. Kenmare, in County Kerry, till lately a bit of a desert for anything more ambitious than a ham sandwich, now has two restaurants with a Michelin star. You can stay in Bantry House with the descendants of the family who built it in the 1720s and gaze at the stunning view over Bantry Bay to Whiddy Island. It must be the only bed-and-breakfast where the drawing room furniture and tapestries belonged to Marie Antoinette.

Dinner at the Butler Arms in Waterville was praised more than the star of Kenmare because of the shellfish straight out of the sea, now appreciated for what it is—the best of its kind. Ballymaloe House, near Cork, deserves its reputation for impeccable food and comfort, and the Shanagarry Pottery next door produces the only wares of that kind I ever want to buy.

The land of a Hundred Thousand Welcomes may not have sun or snow (not enough to slide down anyway), and the sea is too cold to play in, but the beauty of the country, stuffed with history and mystery, plus the rising standards of the hotels, delights people who feel compelled, as we do, to return year after year.

The beauty and the atmosphere of the place stay with me every year, long after I have left Ireland. There, the local newspapers are a continual source of pleasure. Their pictures and headlines are a running commentary on current affairs, which I greatly prefer to their dull English counterparts. The *Cork Examiner* can be relied on for eye-catching stuff like MOUSE IN

BOTTLE OF STOUT and KERRY LADY DEAD IN
DRAIN, neither of which needs much enlargement un-
derneath for the reader to take in what has happened.
But WIVES MAY GET DENTAL BENEFIT from the
Irish Times conjures up lucky husbands grinning to
show off their smart new snappers while their new
wives dare not smile (even if they felt like it) because
of the nasty sights which would be on show. *The
Kerryman* sums up the work of a hospital committee
with NOTHING HAS BEEN DECIDED, while the
Dungarvan Leader's AM I HERE AT ALL? ASKS WA-
TERFORD COUNTY COUNCILLOR poses a basic
question which we must all have asked ourselves at
some time or another. Even *Horse and Hound*, the
trade mag of the Sloane Rangers, has got the drift
when its Irish correspondent heads his column HOW
TO GET FARMERS BACK INTO BREEDING.

My sister Nancy loved the road signs, especially the
ones on the mountain roads which have desperate
twists and turns over the streams. The worst are announced in wasp black and yellow: DANGEROUS
HAIRPIN. More surprising is a big notice on a quiet
stretch of road which says ATTENTION/ACHTUNG.
DRIVE ON LEFT. CONDUIRE A GAUCHE. LINKS
FAHREN. The spot where it is planted is many miles
from any port or airport, so the Franco-German

driver must have got the hang of how to do it, or he would have met his fate long before he arrived on this remote moorland road far from the nearest village. There is a fine new dual carriageway which lets out most of Cork city on the road to the airport. NO PEDESTRIANS, it says, but in the middle of the road is a boy selling evening papers.

Spring and autumn are the seasons of annual general meetings. The older I get, the harder I find it is to sit through them. The words which go with committees, like 'minutes' and 'agenda,' don't exactly send the adrenalin racing, and impatience with a ponderous chairman sometimes makes the affair nearly unbearable. The items on the agenda are slowly ticked off and you pray no one will take up the chairman's suggestion of bringing up something arising out of the minutes. The obligatory thanks to the officers still come as a surprise after all these years. It is such an unsuitable collective word for a group of kindly women who spend much time and energy in raising money for whichever charity the meeting is about. My idea of an officer is anything from a second lieutenant to the colonel of the Coldstream Guards—a far cry

from the good ladies present in the church hall, who
aren't the type to bark out orders on Horse Guards
Parade and would look out of place in bearskins.
When it comes to finding a seconder for the vote of
thanks to the auditor, desperation sets in and I long to
go out in the rain. 'Any Other Business' can be risky,
and it is a great relief when it passes quietly by. Then
comes the speaker, who is, I suppose, meant to in-
struct or entertain and very often does neither, but
spins out the time till the blessed cup of tea looms and
freedom is in sight. If you happen to be the speaker, of
course, things are different and you are in an all-
powerful position. Disappointingly soon, you spot
people crossing and uncrossing their legs, shifting in
their chairs, and searching in the depths of a bag for
the key to the car. All of which makes for a general
feeling of unease and means that the audience is
thankful you forgot the second half of what you were
going to say. If it is a talk with slides, the audience is
in the dark, so you can't see signs of restlessness. Snor-
ing is their only weapon, but they are your victims,
imprisoned in rows till the last click of the projector.
Their patience is an example to us all.

After the annual meeting comes the annual report.
These arrive in our house by the ton, sent by every
known organisation from Barnado's to Bloodstock via
the Water Board and the National Gallery. I suppose

their production gives work for growers of trees, man-
ufacturers of paper, photographers, designers, the people who write them, and the post office. That's good,
but 99 percent of the wretched things represent a huge
waste of time and money, written as they are in un-
readable official language and printed on reams of
shiny, expensive paper. Annual reports published for
their shareholders by public companies vie with one
another in richness of appearance and sheer weight. I
guess the shareholders would prefer a Churchillian
single sheet with the glad or sad news of the company's results, so the money saved could go towards
higher dividends. But it is a question of keeping up
with the Joneses, so no respectable company would
agree to such lack of pomp. I have discovered one exception. It is the annual report of the National Heritage Memorial Fund. If you have had enough of
heritage—English, Living, Built, Landscape, World,
Garden, and the Department of National—do swal-
low your objection to the overworked word and have
a look. The beauty of it is its clarity; never an extra
word, everything is straight to the point. Instead of
the usual rigmarole about financial resources or fund-
ing, even the taboo word 'money' is used every now
and again. The organisation itself must be unique, in
that it has more trustees than staff, who, believe it or
not, number seven. When you have taken in that
amazing fact, start reading, and you will see what I

mean. The descriptions of jewels, woods, paintings, manuscripts, a shingle beach, a fairground king's living wagon, a bit of the Brecon Beacons, a tractor, a colliery, drawings by Gainsborough, Raphael, and Co., Somerset cornfields, several church interiors, a trades union banner, a smashing portrait by Lawrence, a croft in Caithness, garden tools, and an organ which have received grants are a delight. The accompanying photographs of such disparate beneficiaries make one pleased to be a taxpayer. No government department, no waste, no messing about; the grants they can give go straight to these diverse and needy places and things. And now their money is to be reduced from £12 million to £7 million. Remind yourself, please, that the fund was established as a memorial to those who have died for this country. Their number has not diminished. Roll on the National Lottery and may the NHMF get a whopping share of whatever is going. Meanwhile, congratulations to Lord Rothschild, chairman, and Georgina Naylor, director, for the work they do for us.

As a regular listener to the early-morning programme on Radio 4 called 'Today,' I am fascinated by the fact that the people who are interviewed find it impossible to answer a question with a simple yes or no. I except politicians, because woolly answers are their style, but lots of people are quizzed on every subject under the sun, and they all hover about uncertainly. The last few mornings, I have written down the replies which mean yes but are more complicated. Here are some of the most often repeated: 'certainly,' or, to spin it out a bit, 'most certainly'; 'I agree'; 'exactly'; 'indeed,' or, playing for time while they are pondering what they might be asked next, 'indeed that is so'; 'absolutely' ('absolutely' is rather new but is getting more common); 'you're right'—'that's right'—'that's perfectly right'—or just the fashionable 'right,' 'true,' or 'very true'; 'definitely'; 'of course'; 'very much so'; 'precisely'; and 'I hope so' with a little laugh and the emphasis on 'hope.' How I long for someone to say yes, if that is what is meant. It would have the advantage of surprising the cruel questioner so much, he would be silenced. The radio abhors a vacuum—so does an interviewer. I shall keep listening and perhaps one morning someone will manage it. But the ultimate joy would be to hear the answer 'I don't know.'

The world of consultants, which has appeared out of nowhere in the last few years, is a thriving offshoot of whichever trade or industry it professes to know all about. Not so long ago, professionals were trained in their profession, and it would have been an insult to suggest that an outsider probe into the affairs of a company.

Not so now that consultants have arrived. Investing in a new enterprise, or upgrading an old one, be it a restaurant to feed visitors at Chatsworth or arrangements to ease the flow of customers round our Farm Shop, is extremely expensive, so it is thought prudent to consult a consultant before plunging into the unknown. Women's intuition is not to be trusted. The consultant is the one to go by.

He arrives from London, first class on the train, with a couple of acolytes, consultants in the making. Most probably he has never been this far north, so the geography and the ways of the locals have to be explained, all taking his valuable time. After a suitable pause of a few weeks (he is very busy being consulted), a beautiful book arrives, telling you what you spent the day telling him. It is written on paper, about which he has consulted a consultant. The paper consultant has consulted a design consultant, and someone deep in an office has drawn a logo, without which no self-respecting consultant can practise his consultancy.

The result is a ream of paper the size of a tennis court, logo to the fore, and the address (which you might conceivably want) flanked by telephone, telex, and fax numbers in fairy writing at the bottom.

You and your colleagues spend some time translating the book into plain English. You meet to discuss it and decide to do what you thought of doing before going to the consultant.

Almost at once, a huge bill arrives, topped up by first-class travel expenses and more meals than you can imagine three men could possibly eat in a day. It has all added considerably to the cost, but you pay with the comfortable feeling that you have consulted the best consultant in the business.

The word 'luxury' seems to be bandied about in a curious way these days. People's ideas of what it means vary enormously. I'm never quite sure what a 'luxury flat' is, though I believe it should have running water and a radiator or two. Better than not having them, I admit, but what is *real* luxury?

For me, a winter weekend sticks in the memory. I was staying with an artist and his wife in Dorset. I can't remember if there was central heating, but I do remember my hostess coming into my room before breakfast, her head tied in a duster like Miss Moppet, laying and lighting a coal fire for her guest to dress by.

If you've never dressed in front of a coal fire, you don't know what luxury is. They also had half a cow—the farmer had the other half—which meant they had not only proper cream but real butter, a rare commodity indeed.

I can't help comparing that house with many bigger, richer, electric-fired households, some of which are the centre of hundreds of acres of their own farms, milking big herds of cows. But no one can be bothered to skim and churn, and thereby profit from what they own by producing what is described in old-fashioned cookery books as 'best butter.' My Dorset friends win the luxury stakes hands down. A coal fire, half an acre, and half a cow, that's the thing.

A new word which is used to described anything from houses to holidays is 'affordable.' Surely what Lord Lloyd Webber and an unemployed miner can afford are not the same, yet it is trotted out as equally applicable to all. I imagine it means cheap, so why not say so?

The other day, I went to Harrods to look for a coat for a friend who can't go shopping. After all these years, I still miss the bank on the ground floor, and the green leather seats where my sisters and I used to meet and sit and talk and laugh so loudly that the other customers got annoyed. Now there is a slippery marble floor, and fierce young ladies sell all the same makeup things under different names. You can't talk and you certainly don't feel like laughing. But it was what happened outside that struck me as so odd. It was pelting with rain and a gale was blowing, people's umbrellas turning inside out like Flying Robert's in *Struwwelpeter*. A smart car with a chauffeur drew up and an old, cross, rich couple got out. The woman had a mink coat slung over her shoulders, which fell into the road and the dirty water. The commissionaire dashed to pick it up, shook it, and hung it on her again. He opened the door for her and her beastly husband, who didn't lift a finger to help. She walked straight through without looking round. 'Didn't that woman say thank you?' I asked the commissionaire. 'Oh no,' he answered, 'they never do.'

Packaging has gone too far, and the simplest things have become impossible to open. If you buy a toothbrush or a pen or tweezers, you need a strong and sharp pair of scissors to cut through the armour plating of plastic which encases them. No house has enough scissors, so you go out and buy some. But they are similarly encapsulated in a thick shiny film, which human hands and nails are not designed to penetrate. You pull, drag, stamp, and bite, but to no avail. You can see your longed-for object in its close-fitting jacket, shining and clean, which makes it all the more desirable, but there is no hope of getting at it. You buy another pair of scissors and another, till they are ranged alongside the things they are meant to open. If there is a scissor-package opener lurking among the terrifying objects in John Bell and Croyden, you may be sure it will be aseptically sealed, so only a scalpel will do the job.

A few days after this piece was published, an anonymous scalpel arrived by post and happiness set in.

Buying water in bottles to drink at home must be one of the oddest crazes of the last few years. All right, I know London water tastes horrible, and Nanny would say, 'Don't touch it, darling; you don't know where it's been' (sometimes they tell us where it's been, which proves Nanny to be right), but most water tastes the same as the bottled kind and is perfectly good just as it comes out of the tap. Beautiful pictures on the labels and names which conjure up moorland streams, most likely to be stuffed with liver fluke, appeal to the gullible shoppers. Once bought, the heavy bottles have to be lugged back to the car, as there is not much pleasure in a guilty gulp of water in the shop. The choice seems endless. Bottles of all shapes and sizes and even colours (the blue one is very pretty) fill the shelves of grocers' shops already given over as much to dog, cat, and bird food as that for humans. I suppose people will soon be buying water for pets, or they will be accused of discriminating against them. Think of the number of lorries carrying this extraordinary cargo all over the country, getting in the way of things that matter, like you and me going for a spin. But the astonishing thing is the price. Please note that milk costs 43p a litre (it averages 23p to the farmer, by the way), petrol is a little over 50p a litre, and still water, would you believe it, costs up to 79p for the same quantity. As a shopkeeper, I must think up some other pointless commodities with which to fuddle the good old public.

We have heard a lot lately about two men sharing a bed in a French hotel and the usual speculation as to what may have happened in it.* You have only to go a little way back to discover that travellers often had to share a bed, whether they chose to or not. In the 1750s, Henry Cavendish, the famous scientist, and his brother Frederick journeyed to Paris together. When they arrived in Calais, they stopped at an inn and had to sleep in a room where someone was already in bed. It was a corpse laid out for burial. (The Cavendish family were famed for silence until a timely injection of Cecil blood in the last generation set them talking more than most.) Lord Brougham wrote of Henry, 'He probably uttered fewer words in the course of his life than any man who lived to fourscore years and ten, not excepting the monks of La Trappe.' Nothing was said by the laconic pair till they were well on the road next morning. Eventually, Frederick said, 'Brother, did you see?' 'Yes, I did, brother,' Henry answered. Just think what would happen now. First, the hotel manager would be sent for and given a dressing-down, as he often is by spoilt travellers who don't like finding a dead person in their room. Then the rich headlines would follow: DUKE'S NEPHEWS PRACTISE NECROPHILIA IN FRENCH HOTEL. And there is the question of incest . . .

---

*David Ashby, MP for Leicestershire NW 1983–1997, had shared a hotel bed with a male friend whilst on holiday, as an economy measure. Both denied any homosexual relationship.

The other day, I was on my way to London airport, ridiculously early for the plane, as usual. I stopped to fortify myself for the journey by looking round Chiswick House.* It never disappoints or fails to inspire and fill the observer with wonder. It was a horrible day and the only other people were a party of Americans, the most knowledgeable acting as guide. One asked, 'Which is the portrait of Pope?' The woman said, 'There he is. You can always tell Alexander Pope. He's kinda skinny.'

Journalists and even ordinary people have a strange new habit of leaving out the Christian name when writing about women. It immediately turns the subject into a different person. I cannot recognise my sisters Nancy and Diana as Mitford and Mosley, or another sister when she becomes Treuhaft (though she is sometimes Mitford, too, and then confusion reigns). And

*Chiswick House, one of the first Palladian houses in England, was built and furnished by the third Earl of Burlington and William Kent, circa 1727. It was a property of the Dukes of Devonshire from 1753 until it was sold in 1929.

something unnatural happens to that most feminine of human beings, the American ambassador to France, when she is referred to so baldly as Harriman. I think it started a few years ago with criminals. Somehow it is all right for Hindley and other murderesses, as they hardly deserve a Christian name anyway, but it is extremely muddling when applied to normal women. I don't mind about Thatcher, Bottomley, and Beckett. Having chosen the dotty career of politics, which turns them into Aunt Sallys from the day they were elected, they can stand up for themselves. Must we now drop the Aunt? If so, Sally is no good alone, and anyway, we're back to a Christian name. What a conundrum. I can't see why the reporters do it. It surely isn't to save space—just look at the acres of paper they have to cover with something: acres which become hectares on Sundays. Perhaps it is to do with them not liking the idea of women being proper women. The female journalists are very quaint and contrary, so we can expect something outlandish from them. I suppose it doesn't matter much, but when Hillary is in the news and she turns into Clinton, it does make one blink a bit.

Can we do away with: women who want to join men's clubs, *Cupressus leylandii*, bits of paper that fall

out of magazines and, lately, bits of paper which fall
out of those bits of paper, people who say (and write)
'talking with' when they mean 'to,' flowers in fireplaces, magpies, writing paper with the address at the
bottom or, worse, the American trick of putting the
address on the back of the envelope, which you throw
away and then have to retrieve, female weather fore-
casters, drivers who slow down to go over cattle grids,
hotel coat hangers, Canada geese, 'partners,' liquid
soap machines where the thing you press to get the
stuff out is invisible, sparrow hawks, audience partici-
pation, punning newspaper headlines, and locked
gates? And can we bring back: scythes, sharps, and
middlings, Invalid Bovril, brogues, mourning, silence,
housewives, telegrams, spring cleaning, snow in January instead of at lambing time, nurses in uniform,
muffins, the 1662 prayer book, pinafores for little
boys, fish shops, Bud Flanagan, Ethel Merman, and
Elvis Presley?

The television and the radio delight in feeding a mor-
bid interest in illness and accidents with an ever-
increasing number of programmes showing frightful
things happening to people. Green-clad surgeons getting their heads and hands together over some bit of

body, stretchers bringing a harvest of victims of horri-
fying accidents, and a difficult birth or two vie with
one another to delight us. Turning on the radio, hoping for a cheery tune, I heard, 'Yes, blood blisters on
the roof of the mouth can be very unpleasant.' I
should jolly well think they could, but blood blisters
are the least of the horrors on offer. If you happen to
be even vaguely well, you feel guilty because you
aren't suffering like these unfortunates. Switch the
thing off, you say. Well, of course, that's right. But lots
of people must enjoy such ghoulish entertainment, or
it wouldn't be broadcast.

I notice the heavy (literally) newspapers have their individual ways with obituaries. *The Times* usually
writes at length about a black American jazz musician
who may, or may not, have played in a band with Fats
Waller (of blessed memory). They sometimes throw in
a grey-faced scientist from Eastern Europe who knew
all about some abstruse speciality, a closed book to
lesser mortals.

The *Daily Telegraph* describes the deeds of war he-
roes, illustrated with photos of these handsome men
when in their twenties, smart as paint in uniform,
with straight partings in their thick hair. The descrip-

tions of their gallantry in winning DSOs, MCs, and DFCs with a bar or two read like thrillers and make one marvel that they survived into their eighties.

The *Guardian* recalls many a dreary politician and their boring, worthy lives, and sometimes one of the judges who make headlines by a surprising judgement or the classic questions only judges dare ask, like 'What is a Land Rover?'

The *Independent* goes steadily about its business and can be relied on for accuracy and funniness, usually lacking in others. Few can resist a fashionable dig at the deceased. The smallest peccadillo is dragged up and enlarged upon in an otherwise blameless life devoted to public service.

The tabloids shout out about everyone, however obscure, in show business or sport. They reserve space to report some particularly grisly kind of death met by these unfortunate people. Perhaps they don't count as an obituary, but are just the usual reporting of the daily horror stories.

The specialist magazines are the most rewarding. The *Poultry World* and the British Goat Society's *Monthly Journal* sometimes produce a winner, but my favourite appeared in *Horse and Hound* in the days when foxhunting was perfectly all right.

It began: 'So Beatrice has galloped over and taken the last fence into the great unknown,' and went on to describe the life of an indomitable countrywoman wedded to field sports, one of that special breed which exists only in these islands. It ended: 'Gallop on blithe spirit, and may you find your heaven in a good grass country.'

I hope she did, and I hope there is still no plough in heaven.

There is something mysterious about bread. I don't mean pale, floppy loaves steamed to death by 'bakers,' but the homemade sort, mixed, kneaded, and cooked by human hand in a real oven.

Bread is uncertain, in that the same recipe followed by different people produces very different versions of the 'staff of life.' Perhaps it is something to do with the yeast, alive and almost kicking. Perhaps this magic agent reacts to the mood of the bread maker or the oven. Whatever the reason, the variations are very much part of the charm.

Children who have never tried homemade bread are apt to fall upon it and devour slice after slice, ending with a deeply satisfied sigh and 'I can't eat another thing. I'm full.'

Fancy recipes with different tastes, from herbs and bananas to tomatoes and olives, are easy to surprise people with but are no good for everyday fare. For the best treat, you should wait till August to beg some wheat straight off the combine harvester, put it through the coffee grinder, and see if the resulting bread is not a revelation.

To be in the swim, you must change your name. Steel has turned into Corus, which makes you think vaguely of singing, but I bet the steelworkers don't feel much like singing just now; Woolworth suddenly became Kingfisher, a flash of blue on a quiet river and not exactly the image of the old sixpenny high-street stores. Now the post office is to be called something so odd—not a real name but a concoction of letters, like the name of a film star's baby—that I've already forgotten what it is. I suppose stamps and postmen will go the same way. The Royal Commission on Historical Manuscripts is to drop the Royal (of course) and twist itself round till it becomes the Historical Manuscripts Commission. I wonder if that is sharp enough for 2001. Why not call it the Pony Club or the Delphinium Commission? Then it might make an impact. They say that the V & A is threatening to follow this extraordinary fashion because it used to get confused with the clothes shop C & A. I can hardly be-

lieve this. If true, what will Victoria & Albert turn
into? Maskelyne & Devant? No, that is out of date.
Morecambe & Wise, more likely. And I'm longing to
know what the National Gallery will choose, and Wa-
terloo Station, the Royal Observatory, Madame Tus-
saud's, and the rest of the institutions we were
brought up with. I fervently hope that John Lewis and
Peter Jones won't turn into the Two Ronnies.* I love
all four too much to contemplate it. Chatsworth has
been lumbered with the same name for 450 years,
which is far too long. It is time for a change. Sugges-
tions on a postcard, please.

 There are some rare treats to come.
Elvis is back with a bang and can be
seen in all the big cities in a tour beginning in Newcastle. This incredible
show is a deeply moving experience—I
know because it came to this country last year. There
he is on a vast screen in a vast arena, thousands of

*John Lewis and Peter Jones are my favourite department stores;
Maskelyne and Devant were a team of magicians; Morecambe and
Wise and the Two Ronnies were both comedy duos.

fans gazing at his beautiful face and inspired by his extraordinary voice. As if this wasn't enough, his real old band surrounds the screen, playing live—the inimitable pianist, the guitarist, the wild drummer, and the rest. The Sweet Inspirations, the singers who accompanied him, take clothes a few sizes bigger than in the olden days, but they still make everyone feel happy. It is the man himself who dominates, as he always did, and the adoring fans drink it in, knowing every word and every gesture, unable to sit still in their seats, till the whole arena erupts in clapping and shouting to celebrate the greatest entertainer ever to walk on a stage. ELVIS LIVES. He is often seen in supermarkets. I wish he would call at our London Farm Shop in Elizabeth Street.

Last week, I had lunch with three friends, two of whom live abroad and come to London about once a year. The talk ranged over all kinds of subjects, and it is refreshing to discover how untouched they are by the pounding of the media. They have never heard of Jeffrey Archer ('Is he one of the Archers?'); think a microwave is something to do with hairdressing; mix up Laura Ashley with sex-change April of that ilk; and ask if Cecil Parkinson* is a photographer (vague memories of Norman and Beaton, no doubt). Hoping for even more surprising gaps in their general knowledge test, my London-dwelling friend and I cast another fly, but this time with no success. They have heard of Mr Blair.

I wonder if it is computers which think up such strange names and addresses for the customers of the firms for which they work. Or is it specially dotty secretaries whose minds are on other things while they write? I should love to know. Some are wildly imaginative and endow the customer with a different character, or even another nationality, from the steady old English people they really are. One mail-order company thinks I am called 'Mr/Ms Hess Of,' the subject of an undiscovered poem by Edward Lear perhaps, or a German ex-royalty. (They have kindly sent me an 'Exceptional Customer Award suitable for framing and displaying in the Hess Of Home.') A friend is the Viscountess Mrrrrrrrrr. She finds it difficult to pronounce and thinks it sounds as if she is getting into a

*A British politician who was often in the news.

cold bath. Another friend, who is an architect, has become Mr Jebb Ariba, which suggests he was born in
Ghana or Nigeria. Liberty's (no upstart mail-order
company here, but an old-established firm, which you
might think would get it right) sent a proper letter on
beautiful paper. Below the date is written 'Duchess
D. E. V., Chatsworth, Chatsworth, Chatsworth, Bakewell, Derbyshire.' It begins 'Dear Sir' and goes on
to describe a dress of 'Tana lawn in a floral print of
particularly feminine style and two colourways.' It
doesn't seem to have occurred to them that a Sir might
prefer trousers. And I know Chatsworth is big, but it
really isn't necessary to repeat it three times, as it is
quite easy to find if mentioned just once. I look forward with interest to more and better names and addresses on the brightly coloured pamphlets which
announce that you've won £25,000. Look closer and
you find that, alas, you are the only person on the list
who has not. Odd.

I know the Turner Prize is stale buns now, as it happened months ago, but I missed it at the time and
have since become fascinated by how it is decided.
Someone at the Tate kindly sent the bits of paper

about it, written in a special language, which is not easy to understand. The photos of the prizewinning works of art don't help much, either. It seems that the prize is given to a 'British artist under fifty for an outstanding exhibition or other presentation of their work in the twelve months preceding 30 June.' It is awarded by a jury consisting of four, or sometimes five, good men and true, and a foreman (sorry, chairman). The jurors have a wonderful opportunity to find the artist guilty and sentence him to a term of no work and generally keeping quiet for however many years his art deserves. Amazingly, instead of doing this, they give him twenty thousand pounds. I'm all for people giving each other twenty thousand pounds as often as possible, but the reason in this case seems so very strange. According to the press release, last year's winner is said to 'play an interesting game with the relationship between art and reality' and has a 'refined sensibility in the handling of materials which range from hardboard and crushed steel to asphalt.' Very nice. In one of his exhibits, according to the foreword of the brochure, 'lurks the gap left by a shifted saucepan lid.' Good. A runner-up showed a glass case called *A Thousand Years*. Inside was a box of houseflies, a piece of rotting meat (I think), and what looks like an electric fly-killer. As the proprietor of a butcher's shop, I am pleased to see the meat, but—oh well. Another runner-up says, 'I access people's worst fears.' A third competitor uses dogs' messes. Dogs' messes *are* my worst fears and too often accessed in this house. There will be lots of fine artist's material when I get a new puppy, so I hope he'll come and give me a hand, to our mutual advantage. And so it goes on—but why drag poor old Turner into it? Channel 4 gives the money for the prize. I like Jon Snow, his ties, and his news, but I think I shall have to give him up for a bit.

Could some clever reader tell me what a quantum leap is and where I can see one performed? Who the chattering classes are and where I can listen to them? And what a learning curve is and how I can climb onto one?

CHATSWORTH

Thirty Years' Progress

 Clearing out a drawer last week, I found the minutes of a meeting held on 6 July 1965. Those present were Tim Burrows (then Currey & Co's secretary to the trustees), Hugo Read (then Chatsworth agent), Dennis Fisher (then comptroller), and myself.

The familiar worries of expenditure exceeding income on house and garden were discussed, and various large jobs needing to be done were listed.

Mr Fisher and Mr Read mentioned the following which would probably require attention in the next four years:

- Greenhouses—repairs and renewal of heating system.
- Connection of the house to the new main drain.
- Renewal of roof over north side of house sometime in the next twenty years.

Apart from these, and the possible redecoration of the library, they 'could not foresee any major expense for which they would have to call in outside contractors, but emergencies might arise and they thought it would be prudent to allow between seven and ten thousand pounds a year for major items which their own staff could not cope with.' I wonder what we four would have thought had we known then the number of 'special jobs' which have cropped up every year and have been successfully completed since 1965.

The minutes continued:

> Mr Burrows enquired if there was any possibility of increasing the takings from the public. It was agreed that the provision of a café or other catering facilities (which would bring in more money) would not only spoil the present character of the place but would also very likely cause more trouble than it was worth by encouraging people to leave much litter about the gardens.

At that time, the only refreshment provided for our visitors was from the cold tap in the wall by the Lodge, which now carries the notice WATER FOR DOGS.

It was much the same with the shops. The idea was it was unfair, and greedy, to expect people to part with more money than the entrance fee (then five shillings for adults and three shillings, sixpence for children for house and garden). It dawned on me only slowly that people actually wanted to take something away to remind them of their visit and that they were hungry and thirsty as well. Now a lot of people come on purpose to eat and to shop.

Thanks to those who look after the restaurant and the shops, they are generally thought to be the best of their kind. The reason I am bold enough to say this is because of the number of people who ask to come and see how both these thriving departments are run. Not only are we all very proud of them but they are two highly successful businesses, providing what accountants call 'a significant contribution' to the house and the estate.

We have come a long way in thirty years. Perhaps we ought to become consultants!

Memories of Chatsworth in 1950

Andrew and I, Emma, aged seven, and Sto, six, lived in Edensor House with an extraordinary number of domestic staff, squeezed into what are now flats, and a frightening butler, who would tell anyone who would listen that he had known better places. If we had more than three people to stay, they lodged at Moor View (a cottage at the top of the village) and were soon known as the Suicide Squad.* There were horses in the Edensor House stables and the Estate Office was in the upstairs rooms.

There were no cattle grids in the park—hence the wires still above the garden walls at Edensor to prevent the deer helping themselves to flowers and vegetables. Deer, cattle, and sheep regularly wandered out of the park at Edensor and Calton Lees, but they didn't get far because there were always people about on foot or bicycle to herd them back in. Everyone walked or cycled. There were two cars in Edensor— the vicar's and ours.

Meanwhile, Chatsworth was looked after by the comptroller. Ilona and Elizabeth Solymossy, Hungarian sisters, arrived there in 1948. These two, trained as a teacher and a chemist, came to England as refugees in 1938, and worked as cook and housemaid to my sister-in-law Kathleen Hartington (née Kennedy) in her house in Smith Square, London, after she was widowed. Kathleen died in a plane crash in May 1948, and in August that year, my mother-in-law persuaded the sisters to come to Chatsworth to organise

---

*The Suicide Squad was so called because they had to go out on winter nights to another house to bathe and change and return to us for dinner. They had to go out again to bed.

the mammoth task of cleaning the dirty old house in readiness for re-opening to the public in 1949. They, and their Eastern European staff (no English people would do such work at that time),* were well settled here by 1950. They lived in the Bachelor Passage and the Cavendish Passage.

After they had been here a few years, one was less likely to open a drawer and discover, as I once did, a miniature of Duchess Georgiana, a Women's Institute programme of 1932, a bracelet given by Pauline Borghese to the Bachelor Duke to hide a crack in the marble arm of a statue of Venus, and a crystal wireless set.

It was then that I began to realise the extraordinary devotion to the house which had been shown by the comptroller, Mr Shimwell, and his men since the family left in 1939. To the surprise of our advisors later in the 1950s, there was no dry rot, thanks to the vigilance of those years.

I remember five or six joiners, greatly charming and always ready for a chat. What they did all day, I don't know, but the clocks chimed as one on the hour, an eerie sound in the huge empty rooms. Mr Maltby was the head house carpenter, a most loveable character, who had 'put the house away' in eleven days in

*There was a strong feeling against big houses like Chatsworth at that time, and no English people wanted jobs which reminded them of pre-war domestic service.

September 1939 to make it ready for the school which was being evacuated to Chatsworth, and so he was an encyclopaedia of knowledge as to where furniture and all the rest were heaped and whence it came—he remembered where it was placed before the dormitories and classrooms took over in 1939.

The Solymossy sisters used to tie up their heads in dusters, like Beatrix Potter's Miss Moppet, and attack a room at a time, their whole staff working together till it was clean, and then on to the next one. There was a fog of dust everywhere and by afternoon their faces were unrecognisable. They worked very hard, but the rooms remained sadly shabby. There was not only rationing of food and petrol but everything was hedged about with regulations. You had to get a permit to spend £150, the maximum allowed in a year for repairs and redecoration, irrespective of the size of house, so there was no chance of making it look better.

My father-in-law lived alternately at Churchdale* and at Compton Place in Eastbourne and spent the weeks in London, and my mother-in-law always went with him. After Andrew's elder brother, Billy Hartington, was killed in 1944, I never remember my father-

*Churchdale Hall, five miles from Chatsworth, where my parents-in-law lived till the ninth Duke of Devonshire died, and also during World War II.

in-law entering the house at Chatsworth. From time to time, he came to the garden, but that was all.

It was a sad place, cold, dark, empty, and dirty. Even so, there was something compelling in the atmosphere, and it was always an excitement to explore the shuttered rooms, but the spirit of the place had gone and only an incurable optimist could guess it would ever return.

On 26 November 1950, my father-in-law died suddenly while at his favourite occupation of chopping wood in the garden at Compton Place. Andrew was in Australia at the time. He came home to the sadness of losing his father and to worries over the death duties, which affected the lives of so many connected to Chatsworth as well as the immediate family. Nineteen fifty was not a cheerful year for this place.

The Olden Days Brought Up-to-Date . . . and Now

 In the 1970s, the Environment was invented. At Chatsworth, we began to get letters from teachers who had brought their pupils round the house and wanted to take them onto the surrounding land to learn how it was used. Reading their questions and comments brought home to me that what I knew so intimately when I was young was a closed book to most children now.

Ignorance has escalated as 'family farms,' with their mixed livestock, have all but disappeared. Animals and birds are shut away in buildings, and all people see as they dash along the roads are some Friesian cows, a few sheep, and unknown crops, fenced off in fields where humans are not welcome.

In 1973, we decided to set up the Farmyard at Chatsworth, to explain to the children that food is produced by farmers who also look after the land and that the two functions are inextricably mixed.

The milking demonstration is the highlight of the day. The audience remains riveted to the spot, fascinated, shocked, and delighted by this twice-daily ritual. One little boy from the middle of Sheffield said to me, 'It's the most disgusting thing I've ever seen in me life. I'll never drink milk again.'

This reaction is not unusual, but you never know what is going to capture their imagination. A friend who farms in the Home Counties had a party of London children down for the day. He spent hours explaining the theory and practise of dairy farming and finally asked what had interested them most. After much nudging and giggling, one of them said, 'Watching the cows go to the toilet.'

What happens to the milk from the very much tu-berculin- and brucellosis-accredited cows in our Farm-yard? You are not allowed even to give away this dangerous stuff because it has only been cooled, not pasteurised, sterilised, homogenised, or any other 'ised.' If the children had so much as a taste, we should be closed down pronto.

Amazingly, there are not (yet) any regulations for-bidding calves to drink their natural food, so when they have had their share, we, brave as lions, use the rest in the house. What my mother called 'unmurdered milk' is quite different from the bought stuff, which has been through so many different processes it has lost its savour. Our homemade butter and thick cream is a daily delight, and we all seem quite well on it.

It is not only children who are far removed from country matters. Some teachers who visit the Farm-yard are surprised to hear that a cow has to have a calf before she gives milk; they don't connect these two facts of life.

Nor is ignorance of the natural cycle confined to town dwellers. A well-known fund-raiser for rain forests (grown-up) lives deep in the West Country and often passed the garden of a friend of mine who grows dahlias. After the first frost of October, she telephoned my friend in a rage: 'Why have you poisoned the dahlias? They are all dead and horrible and brown.

How could you do such a thing?' (The rain forest lady can never have read Mr Jorrocks's* joyful autumn cry, 'Blister my kidneys, the dahlias are dead!' But then I don't suppose she approves of foxhunting.) Irritated beyond words, my friend answered, 'Yes, and I'm going out now to do the same to all the oaks and beeches round here.'

My husband is an excellent fellow in every way, but he is not a countryman. The grass in the churchyard is an annual problem, as it is in most villages. I suggested putting sheep in. Most suitable, I thought, Lamb of God, Sheep of My Hand, the very thing. 'We can't do that. Everyone will be furious.' 'Why? Isn't it a simple and practical thing to do?' But he was adamant, and another untidy summer passed. When pressed for the real reason, he said, 'Can't you see, it's out of the question—the sheep would lift their legs on the gravestones.'

Our Farmyard is popular (100,000 visitors a year), but it has its critics. A woman brought a party of children who are junior members of an animal welfare organisation. She wrote to tell me they enjoyed the day but that there was a serious objection, because the children were conducting a survey on how the animals are treated as an attraction for the public.

---

*Mr Jorrocks is the principal character in the sporting books of R. S. Surtees, the most famous of which is *Handley Cross*.

They liked the free-range chickens—until the children started their picnic, and then they were exasperated by the close attentions of the chickens and suggested that they should be penned after all. They concluded that the trout in their big tanks were bored and that 'the cluster of people round the rabbit pen put the animals in a predator/prey situation.' I really don't know how to amuse bored trout and cannot cope with human predators, so I broke the rule of a lifetime and did not answer her letter.

Once a year, on Schools' Countryside Day, we expand beyond the Farmyard to cover the whole estate. On Wednesday, 2,500 Derbyshire schoolchildren aged nine to eleven, and their teachers, spent the day in the park and saw the outdoor departments of the estate—farming, forestry, and game—demonstrating their work.

Both teachers and children hear from the men whose lives are spent practising the mysteries of looking after the land and its products. Those of us brought up with them take all this for granted, but the vast majority have little idea of the seasonal toil, which is an endless game of animal, vegetable, and mineral.

Enormous tractors trundle over from our arable farm and bring potatoes, sheaves of wheat, barley, oats, linseed, and oilseed rape. Except in the case of potatoes, few people know the difference between these crops, nor do they know their uses. When the wheat is pointed out, it is vaguely connected with bread, but the rest are a complete mystery.

The gamekeepers' plot is the most popular. The children are fascinated by the pheasant and partridge chicks, mallard ducklings, ferrets, traps (including some old traps, now illegal), and guns. They see clay pigeons shot. Some of the teachers have a try and some of the children say they would like to shoot the teachers. There is pandemonium over bagging the spent cartridge cases.

At the forestry demonstration, Paul, a young forester born and bred at Chatsworth, and Phil explain how woods are planted, weeded, pruned, thinned, and eventually felled and that the cycle is then repeated. Because trees take longer to mature than a human lifetime, it seems difficult to understand that this country's only self-generating raw building material is a crop and has to be 'managed.'

Trees produce the most extreme reactions. Paul told me, 'On seeing the saws, several children re-marked, "Do you enjoy killing trees? Don't you feel guilty? Why don't you blow them up with dynamite; surely that would be quicker? Do you only cut down trees to make money?"'

A head teacher asked: 'Couldn't you let the trees die naturally before you cut them down?' Watching the mechanical tree harvester: 'Don't you use axes anymore?' Paul concluded that neither teachers nor children understood forestry. 'They see it as legalised vandalism. Their idea that we only destroy is based on media coverage of rain forests. A few teachers thought we were pulling the wool over the children's eyes, but others were keen to know more.'

In desperation, the young foresters pointed to the huge panorama all round, with groups of trees young and old and Capability Brown's plantations bordering the park, and asked, 'Do you like what you see?' They answered, 'Yes.' 'Well, that is what we do—we keep it looking like that.'

Those privileged to own land must explain to people who very naturally wish to use it for recreation what it costs in money and people to keep it looking attractive enough for them to want to ride, walk, run, and sit on it. The beauty of the country was largely man-made in the days of cheap labour. Now that we are struggling to maintain the fine balance between man and nature, it would be helpful if walkers and other users understood the price of keeping hedges, stone walls, gates, farm and forest roads, streams, and woods in order. In spite of the ever-thickening fog of bureaucracy, the landowner still has the joy of ownership—but he also has all the responsibility, and those who use the land have none.

The Farmyard, and now Schools' Day, have had an effect on the Chatsworth men who meet the teachers and children. It has been brought home to them that their jobs are not understood by the majority of visitors. Wallers, keepers, drainers, foresters, sawyers, butchers in the Farm Shop, shepherds, tractor drivers, and stock-men—all would like to spend some hours explaining their age-old skills brought sharply up-to-date. But how can they be spared from their jobs? Who is to pay for their time?

Who is to tell visitors that these are the people who make Chatsworth and its surroundings what they are? Chatsworth and similar places could be huge outdoor classrooms, but all any of us can do without encouragement from on high amounts to a drop in the ocean.

We are told that sixty-seven people are leaving agriculture and associated industries every day. Could not some of these, not academics but the real people, return to their roots to teach?

Perhaps it isn't worthwhile. I can see the day coming when gang mowers will cut the grass fields, the arable land will be left to its own thistly devices, and paths through the woods will become impenetrable jungles, for which ramblers will have to be armed with machetes. And then who would be killing the trees? We can drink French milk, eat Argentinian beef, import flour from America and timber from the Baltic. It would save a lot of work.

But I will grow a lettuce by the front door, just to prove I can.

Who are tourists? What are they? You, me, friends, relations, most of the people we know and millions we don't. Why do we tour? What makes people come to Chatsworth?

It is no new phenomenon. The house has been open for people to see round ever since it was built. In the late eighteenth century, the table was laid on 'Open Days' for anyone who wanted dinner.

In 1849, the railway reached Rowsley, three miles away, and brought eighty thousand people to go round the house and garden that summer. The Duke gave instructions that the waterworks be played 'for everyone, without exception.'

Huge crowds visited Chatsworth at the turn of the century on Bank Holiday weekends. The tour of the house and garden was free until 1908, and after that, the fee—one shilling for adults and sixpence for children—was given to the local hospitals. It was not until 1947 that the revenue from the visitors went towards the upkeep of the place.

I have listened and talked to the people who have been coming for nearly fifty years. The points of interest have changed, but the place has not—there is no fun fair and no entertainment except the house and its contents. The same goes for the garden. Perhaps that is why only the genuinely interested come. Vandalism and litter are not problems.

Forty years ago, a regular remark from women seeing the cast-iron fireplaces in the state rooms was 'Look at all that black leading.' Few women under the age of seventy know what black leading is now.

They are still astonished by the size of the house. A girl who complained about the price of a ticket, saying she didn't like paying so much to see a few old-fashioned rooms, reached the end of the tour and said, 'I'm knackered. Bring me a chair.'

Attitudes towards places such as Chatsworth have changed completely in the last fifty years. After the war, there was a strong feeling against privately owned big houses and estates.

In spite of this, people came, if only to criticise. The government's penal taxation laws were gleefully underlined by local government officials, who did their best to make things difficult.

A typical instance was the vociferous lobby, instigated by the socialist MP for West Derbyshire and the chairman of the Derbyshire county council, to bring the A6 through the park, a few yards from the house—an idea which would be unthinkable now.

The public has led the change in attitudes—conservation and preservation are all the rage, and you are suddenly a hero for keeping the roof on; the cries of 'pull it down' from the 1950s and 1960s are long forgotten.

In 1976, the Duke of Bedford wrote a very funny letter to *The Times* about Woburn.* He concluded that 'the average person comes to historic houses because he has bought a car and needs to drive somewhere in it. The number that come for real enlightenment are so few that it is distressing.'

Twenty years on, people want to see works of art. Television programmes such as the *Antiques Roadshow* have sharpened interest in the objects displayed. And when a Jane Austen novel is adapted for television, the briefest glimpse of someone's front door makes it an object of pilgrimage and crowds flock to see the hallowed spot.

A house lived in by the descendants of the family who built it is thought to be more interesting than one belonging to a government department or other organisation, however well presented. There is a keen curiosity about the incumbents.

American visitors find it impossible to believe that

*Woburn Abbey, in Bedfordshire, the seat of the Duke of Bedford (see page 162).

anyone actually lives in this Derbyshire Disneyland. Children ask, 'Have they got satellite telly? Do they wear crowns? Was the Duchess a girl groom?'

They are shocked by Laguerre's naked figures on the painted ceilings and think them out of place in such a posh house.

I am often asked if we mind the lack of privacy during the summer months. On the contrary, I should mind if no one came. Chatsworth needs people to bring it to life.

We are lucky in that the place is so big, there is space for all. It is so well built that when the state rooms are full of visitors, you can sit in our part of the house, below, unaware there is anyone about. When it re-opens every spring, it is intensely pleasing to be able to show people the results of our winter's work.

Some visitors make surprising statements. There is a portrait of me by Lucian Freud, painted when I was thirty-four. It is said to be not exactly flattering. A woman was overheard saying in a gloomy voice, 'That's the Dowager Duchess.' Then, even gloomier: 'It was taken the year she died.'

A man, looking at Sargent's picture of the Acheson sisters in their exquisite long white dresses of the Belle Epoque, said to his wife, 'Those are the Mitford girls. It is extraordinary to think two of them are still alive.' It certainly is. It was painted in 1901.

And I didn't know whether to be pleased or sorry when someone said to a warden, 'I saw the Duchess in the garden. She looked quite normal, really.'

The view from here is beautiful. Looking out of my window over the garden and the river to the park and the woods is a pleasure I never cease to enjoy. There are no telegraph poles, no concrete edges to the road, no double yellow lines, nor anything else vexatious to the eye. The people who come to walk here, like Lowry figures, give scale to the landscape. They lean on the parapet of the bridge, gazing at the view from the opposite angle.

Morning and evening, the park is empty of people, and the sheep and deer become its undisturbed tenants. On stormy days, these ruminants are like weather vanes, telling you the direction of the wind as they choose to lie down in the lea of this hill or that. On the first hot day of the year, the ewes crowd together under a tree for shade like old women at a meeting, and you know that spring has truly come.

Talking of sheep, the other day I needed a simple technical guide to the native breeds (over fifty of them). I rang up my friend, the secretary of the National Sheep Association, to ask if he had an idiot's pamphlet on the subject. 'Yes,' he said, 'we produced one for the

Food and Farming Exhibition in Hyde Park in 1989.'
A gripping read it turned out to be.

The meaning of the words in the glossary stumped
even language experts among my friends, like Paddy
Leigh Fermor and Jim Lees-Milne. One sheep disease
has regional names of intriguing diversity: Sturfy,
bleb, turnstick, paterish, goggles, dunt, and pendro
are all gid. I looked up gid. No luck—it isn't there.
You, Dear Reader, are expected to know exactly what
gid is, and I'm quite sure that you do.

In church at Edensor, while the glorious language of the 1662 prayer
book, with its messages of mystery
and imagination, fills the air, I find my
mind wandering back to the Oxford-
shire churches of my childhood, first at Asthall and
then at Swinbrook, where the same language was spo-
ken in different surroundings.

Both St Mary's Swinbrook and St Peter's Edensor
have seventeenth-century memorials which are worth
going a long way to see. At Swinbrook, they com-
memorate two generations of the Fettiplace family,
who owned the surrounding land till the male line
died out in the nineteenth century. The subjects, who
are weighed down by stone armour and lie stiffly on
their sides, are of about the same date and as arrest-

ingly beautiful as the memorial to Bess of Hardwick's* Cavendish sons in Edensor church.

The feel, smell, and taste of the oak pews at Swinbrook (I suppose that all children lick pews under
cover of praying for their guinea pigs) are not the
same as those at Edensor. They were put in by my father, who paid for them with the money he won by
backing a long-priced Grand National winner owned
by a cousin. He wanted a horse's head carved on the
end of each one, but the bishop would not allow such
frivolity, which was hypocritical of him, as I am sure
he knew the source of my father's bounty perfectly
well.

Sixty-six years ago, my sister Diana, aged fourteen,
played the organ at Asthall. She thought any tune
would do for the voluntary as long as it was played
slowly enough. 'Tea for Two' was repeated again and
again, unrecognised (or so she says), while the congre-
gation waited for the moment when the Venite was
sung to more predictable music. We don't get those
surprises at Edensor because we have a proper organ-

---

*Elizabeth, Countess of Shrewsbury (c. 1527–1608). She married as
her second husband Sir William Cavendish, who purchased the estate of Chatsworth. Widowed in four marriages, she inherited her
successive husbands' estates and indulged her passion for building,
including a house on the site of the present Chatsworth, and Hardwick Hall.

ist. The sermons are preached in the parson's own voice, not a put-on holy one. They are the best I have ever heard.

Now Christmas is upon us again. Everyone is a year older, and there will be some new actors in the Nativity play, which is given by the Pilsley schoolchildren in the Painted Hall at Chatsworth (the audience has outgrown the chapel). The furious faces of some of the older boys, with their dishcloth headdresses and dressing-gown cords all over the place, reflect the expressions of the descendants of the figures they are supposed to represent and whose photographs we see daily in the press.

Thousands of people come to walk in the park at Chatsworth all the year round. There is no way of telling how many, because it is free. Most people enjoy it or, presumably, they wouldn't come, but every now and again a letter of criticism arrives.

Last week, a woman wrote to say she was 'disgusted by the animal faeces on the grass, every few feet' and that she and her grandchildren couldn't play ball games in case of stepping on them. Oh dear. I suppose she wants us to buy a giant Hoover to attach to the JCB* and sweep one thousand acres of well-

*JCB: a British-made earth-moving machine.

stocked ground before breakfast in case she gets her new shoes dirty. Sorry, madam, but you had better go and find some municipally mown grass where your unhappy grandchildren can play their clinically clean games without the fear of stepping on the unspeakable. What a frightful grandmother you must be.

There is nothing like a spot of flattery to cheer you up, especially when it comes in an unexpected and round-about way.

Roy Hattersley is a regular visitor to these parts. When writing a piece for the *Guardian*, he described his dream house, which he discovered when walking in the backwaters of Baslow, a mile or so by footpath from Chatsworth. He felt he could live in it happily ever after. Good.

The house is in a private road. The deputy leader of the Labour Party, taking no notice of the resident of a cottage opposite who challenged him with the classic 'Can I help you?'—meaning, 'What are you doing in this private road?'—gazed lovingly at it through its shrubbery. The straightforward, unfussy square building of local lion-coloured stone is roofed with stout stone tiles and, he said, fits the landscape as naturally as if it had been hewn from the living rock. (It was.) He wondered if it was put up for 'some minor Cavendish functionary or the assistant engineer in a newfangled Victorian water company.' He thought it had the self-confident respectability of a nineteenth-century vicarage, and he liked the fact that it is all of a piece.

Its simple shape was decided upon after looking at a number of drawings of one-sided, overglazed houses with all the other strange variations which make a building look as if it has had a stroke. When presented with a drawing of a house like this one, planners are apt to say, This is all right, but what we should like to see is a good modern building. Anyway, I am very glad Mr Hattersley likes this house. So do I. We built it in 1972.

Camellias

 At Chatsworth, you can find examples of most styles and dates of gardening represented somewhere in its 105 acres. Our situation on the edge of the Pennines, five hundred feet above sea level, and the resulting harsh climate dictate that only the hardiest plants succeed out-of-doors. For this reason, the glasshouses are of vital importance. Nowadays, they are best known for the Muscat of

Alexandria grapes in the autumn and camellias in the early spring.

The spring here is often disappointing. Even in April, there can be frost and snow, so it is then that the frost-free 'cold' houses full of camellias come into their own; their brilliant colours and perfect form, untouched by weather, are an ever-cheering sight. When you go through the glass door and get out of the wind, you find yourself in another world: 'the eternal calm of the greenhouse.'

Camellias have been grown here for over 150 years. Joseph Paxton, gardener, engineer, and builder, was appointed head gardener at Chatsworth in 1826, when he was only twenty-three. He was an innovator and passed on his enthusiasm for all things new to his employer and friend, the sixth 'Bachelor' Duke of Devonshire. The Duke describes himself as having been 'bit by gardening' and was easily persuaded to finance expeditions to the East and to America to bring back plants, many hitherto unknown in this country, to furnish his greenhouses. Among his favourites were camellias.

The stars of the collection are a pair of *C. reticulata* Captain Rawes variety—called after the East India Company captain who brought them back from China. They were planted in the 1840s in the central and highest part of Paxton's Conservative Wall (so called because it conserves heat), a glass case which runs 331 feet up the hillside. At a height of three feet, the trunks are two feet, five inches in circumference, and the camellias reached the twenty-six-foot-high glass roof many years ago. Who knows how tall they would be had the roof grown with them. Between them is the pure white double *C. japonica* Alba Plena.

In early spring, the huge semi-double rose pink flowers of these camellias, with their waxy petals and gold stamens, look so exotic, you wonder if they are real. People stop and stare, and I have often heard them say, 'They must be plastic.' In a good year, the wall seems to be solid rose pink, so close are the flowers.

Andrew and I were married in London in April 1941. The air raids were very bad during the week before our wedding, and the windows of my father's house, where the reception was to be held, were blown out. The rooms looked bleak, but my mother nailed up folded wallpaper as mock curtains and my mother-in-law sent a mass of these astonishing blooms, which, thankfully, saved the day in drab wartime London.

Thanks to the people who look after them, Chatsworth has had many successes at the Royal Horticultural Society Camellia Show in London. Competition is getting hotter every year, but Ian Webster, who is in charge of the greenhouses, wins his share and more of first prizes. A regular winner is the bloodred Mathotiana Rubra, a variety which is difficult to strike from cuttings, so we see our small tree as producing rather rare flowers. I have known this plant for fifty years, and it never fails to perform in March. There are a bewildering number of varieties now. New ones are listed every year, but I still like the old ones best. The simple white flower of Alba Simplex is the essence of purity. I love the old-fashioned pink-and-white-striped *japonica*s and the precise way the petals of the formal doubles are arranged, like flowers in a Victorian bouquet. Andrew's favourites are Jupiter, a single *japonica* of intense red, and Mrs D. W. Davies, blush pink with waxy flowers six inches across. The aptly named rose-form doubles could easily be mistaken for the striped *Rosa mundi*—till you remember the time of year. The earliest to flower is *C. sasanqua*. It is a welcome sight in November and has the advantage of being slightly scented. A succession of camellias are the only decoration we have on the dining table from December to April, but such is their beauty and variety that you could never tire of them. They are arranged on a silver plate, so you look down into the flowers. We use a round table when we are alone, but if there is a party, we put several plates of flowers down the length of the bigger table. They make a brilliant effect, with the pink and red tones picking up the colours in the curtains and carpet of the dining room. Ian Webster arranges them in a one-inch layer of oasis in the bottom of the plate, adding just enough water to soak it. He covers the oasis with camellia leaves, then cuts the flowers with just enough stalk to go into the oasis, so the blooms rest on the leaves. (Be careful when handling the flowers, by the way, as they bruise very easily.) Small trees in tubs also come indoors, but for short periods only, as they're not keen on the dry atmosphere in the house.

Jean-Pierre Béraud—
10 July 1956—13 October 1996

Last year on one of those rare October days which take you back to summer and make it impossible to believe in the coming winter, Jean-Pierre Béraud was killed in an accident. He was forty.

His death had a chilling effect on Chatsworth. People went about their work in a daze. For a long time we could not believe that so vital a man had gone forever. One cannot imagine what this tragedy meant to Diane, their boys, his French family, and his loyal staff.

Jean-Pierre made an unforgettable impression on everyone he met. The proof of the loss that was felt was the number of letters I had from my family, friends, acquaintances, and strangers. The Prince of Wales, the Lord Lieutenant, the High Sheriff, the chief executives of companies who had dined in the Carriage House, heads of local government, distinguished chefs, and people I have never met wrote to me as if I had lost a member of my family.

The story of how a young man from the suburbs of Paris came to England and made his name and his home at Chatsworth is an unlikely one.

My younger daughter Sophy and others were disappointed with our food. She said, 'Why don't you ask Aunt Diana [Mosley] to find someone in Paris who might like it here and who can really cook?' At that time, my sister had a flat over a famous restaurant, Chez Pauline in the Rue Villedo. She asked the *patron* if he knew a young cook who would consider the job. No, he did not. A week later, he told her a boy called Jean-Pierre wanted to go to England—but he had already left. My sister got his home address near Paris, and, strangely enough, his parents lived not far away from her.

Then Jerry comes into the story. Jerry is an old family friend who has been butler/driver with the Mosleys for over forty years. He guessed the Bérauds would have no telephone and so took a note from my sister to their flat in Palaiseau. Madame Béraud gave him the address of a hotel in Portman Square where Jean-Pierre had found work. My sister and Jerry were to go to London the next day. Jerry wrote:

Lady Mosley and I went along to the hotel one afternoon to see if I could find him. They said he was on duty but after some persuasion they went and got him. He met Lady Mosley outside the hotel in the car and it was arranged that when he finished his duties I would return and pick him up and take him to Chesterfield Street to meet you. The rest I am sure you know. Going up to Chatsworth must have seemed a million miles for Alan and Jean-Pierre—not being able to have a conversation.

The next time I saw him was at Chatsworth, where he had laid out a wonderful tea tray in his room, and I could see from the happiness in his face that he had fallen in love with Chatsworth. *Shasworth* as he used to pronounce it, with his French accent and his lisp. He talked and talked about *Shasworth* and the Duchess and Duke. I only wish I had had a tape recorder that day. After that meeting, we became good friends. He told me something which I will al-

ways remember. He said he was having difficulty with somebody and he was longing to discuss it with the Duchess. He compared it to if
you wanted to see God—you had to get St Peter's approval. So he said one day he had decided why go to St Peter when he could go
straight to God!

The last time I saw him was at Mrs Jackson's* funeral. We had a chat and he was still
delighted with how Chatsworth was developing.
He said he would talk about it again, but . . .

When Jerry brought Jean-Pierre to Chesterfield Street
for the interview, one of my sons-in-law came to
translate, because, to my shame, I can't speak French.
I learnt that he had worked in some of the best restaurants in Paris since he was thirteen years old. He was
now twenty-two. I asked him if he could make *sauce
béarnaise*. He gave me a pitying look, and I realised I
had made a gaffe.

In spite of this unpromising start, he agreed to
come to Chatsworth for three months. I think he
would have clutched at any straw to escape from the
hotel kitchen, where there was not one Englishman—
and he had come to London to learn English.

*Pamela Jackson, née Mitford, my sister.

From the day he arrived, we were reminded what good food is. I had to act out 'cabbage' and everything else till he learnt enough English for us to communicate the essentials to each other.

His ambition was to go to America and seek his fortune. We talked about it, and, through my sister-in-law, I found what seemed to be a suitable job for him. He left Chatsworth, and we missed him. Soon after he had started work in New York and the Bahamas, the Queen and Prince Philip were coming to stay. I rang up his employer and said, 'If I pay his fare, can Jean-Pierre come back and cook for them?' It was arranged. The food was perfect and all went well.

On the Monday morning following, Jean-Pierre came to see me. 'I'm not going back to America,' he said. 'Oh you *must*; it is Mr . . . 's busy season and he's depending on you.' 'I want to stay here,' he repeated. After some argument, he did go back, but not for long. The reason was simple—he had fallen in love with Diane.

Life with Jean-Pierre wasn't all plain sailing. In the early days, he used to burst into my room saying why couldn't he have this and that *at once*, why was everything done so slowly here . . . Derrick Penrose remembers not dissimilar occasions—but Jean-Pierre's temperament and his passion for getting things done made it impossible for him to be calm and wait; it must be *now*. We used to laugh about it afterwards.

He saved the Farm Shop from closure when it was suffering losses, setting up the kitchen which turned it to profit, laying the foundation of what it has grown into today. His energy was by no means expended by cooking for two old people and their occasional guests. So, long before he became manager there, he made all kinds of things for the Farm Shop and kept exact accounts of every ounce of flour and every minute of his time. One winter, he made three thousand pounds of marmalade by hand to be sold and then stormed into my room, saying he would never cut up another orange. (Mind you, I hadn't asked him to do it.)

When we took the Devonshire Arms Hotel at Bolton Abbey in hand, Jean-Pierre was chef there for some months. There were no proper pots and pans. He didn't wait for a budget from the directors, but dashed to Leeds and bought a *batterie de cuisine* on my personal account. Then he took over the catering for the visitors to Chatsworth—first in the inconvenient west and north bits of the stables. Later, Bob Getty and he designed new kitchens and made the Carriage House into what I believe is acknowledged to be the best restaurant attached to a house which is open to the public.

Bakewell Rotary Club made him a member—a rare honour for a foreigner.

He saw a demand for cooking lessons and, ever

thorough, he attended courses at Prue Leith's in London and the famed Manoir aux Quat' Saisons near Oxford to see how it was done. His lessons were soon booked up and his pupils returned again and again. Filming for a television company was to have started in January . . .

So often I used to say, 'What *are* we going to do?' about whatever was concerning me, and the answer was always the same: '*Don't worry*' (to rhyme with 'lorry').

As well as looking after our kitchen and the Carriage House (which soon made a mighty contribution to estate overheads), he had a thriving business of his own in Matlock, Bakewell, and at Carsington Reservoir. He was on the crest of a wave.

After the disaster, among the marvellous letters I received was this from Peter Day:* 'Cookery is an art but not so much a fine art or an applied art as a performing art, like dancing, acting, or singing. It is of the moment and then gone, and has to be spot on.

'I was struck by this, even awestruck, in Jean-Pierre's case, when the staff and their families were invited to see the big table in the Great Dining Room with all its silver and special decorations ready for the great dinner for the Society of Dilettanti, to which His

*Keeper of the Collection at Chatsworth.

Grace was host. There amid all the wide-eyed admirers strolling round the table were Jean-Pierre and his family—only a minute or two before he had to go down to the kitchen to *cook* this mighty meal in prospect! I think I vaguely thought everything would somehow have been prepared days in advance. But I realised then with a shock how much Jean-Pierre's work (or art) was like going onstage for a great performance and giving his audience an evening of pleasure, a transport of delight—something to get right on the night, every night.

'In his case, his whole life and character were like this, immediate and direct, all passion, with no side, front, or anything else to come between him and others. Everyone who knew him knew that storms were followed instantly by sunshine. Jean-Pierre could not have been more at one with the lively art of which he was master, and memories of him will never be other than vivid.'

Another letter which put the thoughts of all of us into words was from Simon Seligman:* 'I know that you have lost a kindred spirit, a brilliant, creative, and original man. He was like a blazing comet in my life, even in the few years I knew him, so I can imagine some of the loss you must be feeling.'

*Promotions and Education Manager at Chatsworth.

Jean-Pierre was one of the most remarkable men I have ever met. He was a true friend to Chatsworth and to me.

Foot and Mouth Disease 2001

 HOT SOUP says the notice on the road outside the post office in Edensor, the village within the walls of Chatsworth Park. This notice covers the rough lane from Bakewell, which brings walkers past the cottages, built from a Victorian pattern book, to the public road, which runs through the thousand-acre park.

Hot soup and teas in the winter, ice cream and teas in the summer are a major part of Nigel Johnson's business as a sub-postmaster in a small village. Now, like to Eleanor Rigby's grave, nobody comes.

The post office is part of a suddenly forgotten landscape, put voluntarily out of bounds to the thousands of people who come here from Sheffield, Chesterfield, Nottingham, and farther afield to walk in all weathers at all times of the year and to the thousands more who come from all over the world to see the house and garden. Not since 1967 have I looked out of my window and seen no one on the bridge, the focal point of the park, the place where people stand in the afternoon sun to stare at the golden windows which light up the west front of Chatsworth. The bridge is halfway between the north and south entrances to the unfenced acres of grass, where children and dogs are welcome, people can run and shout and play games or picnic by their prams under a tree. This is how it has been during the sixty years I have known the place, and now, suddenly, it is empty, like an early-morning photograph before anyone is about.

I hardly dare write it, but there is no outbreak of foot-and-mouth disease in the immediate neighbourhood, yet this place is changed beyond recognition.

Our house and garden should have been opened to visitors on Wednesday. There has been the usual rush to get everything ready, the place looks immaculate, clean and shining, a new exhibition of twentieth-century works of art has been set up, restoration of sculptures and redecorations are there to be seen, the shops are full of new and exciting things, and the restaurant ovens are waiting to be heated up. But the doors are shut.

The seasonal staff, 166 of them, have been laid off —15 people in the gift shops, 70 catering staff, 66 ticket sellers, car parkers, and wardens. The Farm Shop in Pilsley is open because it is not in the park, but is as quiet as it would be in a January snowstorm, and fifteen assistants have had to go. The free car park in Calton Lees is bound by one of those unclimbable wire builders' fences, almost an insult to the thousands of people who usually use it.

Statistics stare us in the face, but the difficulties affecting the people who have been made redundant are as different as the individuals themselves. They depend on the employment generated by the half million visitors who usually come here over the ensuing seven months, yet these people are miles away from the farmers whose stock is lost and spirits are crushed. All the same, the lives of these Chatsworth employees have been cruelly disrupted.

How long will it last? How long will people stick to the rules? *What are the rules?* No one seems to know. Mixed messages fly through the air. One minister tells us not to go into the country. Another suggests tourists should go to the northwest, presumably to see and smell eighty thousand rotting carcasses. What a way to run a country.

People have been exemplary in respecting the notices asking them not to come to the park, but a fine weekend when the birds are singing and there is a longing to be out-of-doors and to let the children loose on the grass may soon be too strong a temptation for our neighbouring city dwellers wanting fresh air and freedom; till now, these precious commodities have been available here in endless quantity.

Chatsworth house, garden, park, and woods and the farther landscape are as one; the cattle and sheep grazing out-of-doors are as much a part of the place as the Rembrandts are indoors: They support one another to make the whole.

Farming here goes in harmony with nature and the huge numbers of visitors. If the sheep and the deer go—which God forbid—an integral part of the place will go with them. It is the spectre of such a disaster which the people who look after this place are living with in a kind of limbo. And it is repeated all over the country.

Our 4,500 ewes have started lambing: There is usually a cheerful atmosphere in the caravan by the lambing sheds where the veterinary students and other seasonal helpers snatch a quick cup of tea between lambing a ewe in trouble, penning the newborn lambs with their mothers to avoid 'mis-mothering,' and filling the hay racks and water bowls. The necessary precautions are meticulously carried out. It goes without saying that the lambing staff must enter and leave the buildings spotlessly clean, and they have to allow five days between lambing here and going to the next job or back to college. They have their own special car park in the yard, with disinfectant and scrubbing places. Everything is done as efficiently as ever by our magnificent staff, but even Radio 2 is turned off.

Some lambing shepherds traditionally start in the south of the country, where lambs are born earlier in the year, and work their way north to the lowlands of Scotland a couple of months later. This year, there will be no ewes in these areas for them to tend.

Most of the 'cade' lambs—the weakest of triplets or those born to a ewe which has died—are mothered on to a ewe with a single lamb and enough milk for two. But the surplus are sold to people who come from here, there, and everywhere, who bring them up on the bottle. There can be none of that this year—no strangers are allowed near. The cades will be 'tapped on the back of the head' and that will be the end of them.

In our so-called civilised society, we have become used to being more or less in control in everyday life, whether it be in farming, shopkeeping, or opening a house to the public. Now there is fear of the unknown, like a medieval plague.

Politicians come and go on the television between the harrowing scenes of human and animal misery, making things worse with their endless words and wishful thinking and apparent inability to make or implement decisions. Their shiny cars, neat suits, and hateful hairstyles are a world apart from the muddy

Land Rovers, layers of sweaters and waterproofs, and broken faces of the Cumbrian farmers.

An astonishing fact is that none of the recommendations of the Northumberland report written after the 1967 outbreak have been carried out or, apparently, even considered. It seems incredible when you realise those like Lord Plumb, with a lifetime's experience of farming and farming politics, worked for nine months on the Committee of Inquiry after that outbreak. He and his colleagues came to conclusions full of common sense, even down to the details, like the fact that there should be a sufficient number of captive bolt pistols so that pistols could be set aside for cooling without holding up the slaughter.

I very much doubt if Mr Brown* has ever held a gun with a hot barrel, but practical countrymen like those who wrote this report know exactly the sort of problems continual shooting would create.

I wonder if he knows that meat is still imported here from countries where foot-and-mouth is endemic. I wonder if he knows anything.

This same Mr Brown, who is meant to be in charge of agriculture in this country, has not been to the northwest since the epidemic began. Can you imagine

*Nick Brown, then Minister of State for Agriculture, Fisheries, and Food, 1998–2001.

the politicians of old ducking their responsibilities in such a cowardly fashion?

To top up this catalogue of disaster, we are told there will be 'an election' or two elections on 3 May. Everyone I have talked to here agrees it is positively obscene even to consider such a thing while this national emergency is with us.

Here, there is an eerie atmosphere and near silence. Only the Prime Minister goes on talking.

BOOKS AND

COMPANY

Stranded!

I cannot imagine why I was asked to contribute to this series, where you have to choose and describe ten books for company on the Trans-Siberian Railway. I have read very few books and I have minded finishing them so much that I have often vowed not to start another. Coming to the end of some gripping story or reaching the inevitable death of the subject of a biography is like losing a friend whom you have begun to depend upon night and day in a secret liaison with the author. It is no good saying you can read it again. It is never the same the second time.

I imagine that looking out of the train window, hoping to spot a bear or a sable, might pall after you have trundled by the first million birch trees. Russian and Asian birds would be meaningless to one who likes only blackbirds and thrushes, and I imagine the agricultural scenes, fascinating to start with, would be as repetitive as the birches.

So I must think about ten tiresome books and the reasons for choosing and lugging them up the steep steps of the train. (I hope it still looks like the train in the opening scene of the film *Anna Karenina*.)

Books of reference do not have the same trouble with the ending, because you don't read them straight through, so they can't get the hold on you that the other kind do. And when you are old, you forget what you have looked up (and why) and you happily do it all over again. *The Oxford Book of Quotations* will do very well, and I can go on being surprised by the number of everyday sayings from Shakespeare and the Bible. Of course, it has the unfortunate side effect of whetting the appetite for more, but it will keep me happily occupied for many hours. I am at home with our copy, blue cloth cover with dark rings where sloppy wineglasses have been put to rest. So that is book number one.

The second book is short, only 1,237 words (a lesson to the writers of thousand-*page* biographies of dreary politicians which litter the visitors' bedrooms at Chatsworth), small, neat, and light enough to make up for the bulk of my first choice. The print is excellent and the illustrations are second to none. As a shopkeeper, I revere it as the best book on retailing ever written. It is *The Tale of Ginger and Pickles*, by Beatrix Potter. Ginger, the yellow tomcat, and Pickles, the terrier, kept a village shop which stocked most things required by their customers. The shop was patronised by the locals, rabbits, rats, mice, frogs, and tortoises, who lived around Sawrey, in the Lake District, at the turn of the century. The mice were rather frightened of Ginger and the rats were frightened of Pickles. Ginger made Pickles serve the mice, because they made his mouth water and he could hardly bear to see them going out with their little parcels. Pickles felt the same about the rats. But they realised that to eat their customers would be bad for business. The rats shopped extravagantly, and Samuel Whiskers ran up a bill as long as his tail.

In spite of being nervous of the proprietors, all these creatures crowded into the shop and bought a great deal of whatever took their fancy, especially toffee. But Ginger and Pickles made the age-old mistake of giving unlimited credit. Nobody paid and there was nothing in the till. They could not afford to buy food for themselves and had to eat their own goods—biscuits and dried haddock—after the shop was shut.

The ever-present village policeman (oh, where is he now?) terrified Pickles, because there was no money to buy himself a dog licence. Tabitha Twitchit ran the other shop in the village and insisted on cash down. In spite of stocking less attractive goods, she prospered.

Things at Ginger and Pickles's went from bad to

worse. Eventually, they went bankrupt, shut up shop, and retired. Nobody cared. Tabitha Twitchit, now a one-cat monopoly, put everything up a halfpenny. Pickles became a gamekeeper and Ginger, surrounded by the latest in traps and snares, grew stout in a rabbit warren. Thus they got their own back on their debtors. The watercolour of Pickles in his new job, carrying a gun, his long-nosed face peering round a wall, in pursuit of the rabbits who had found the counter to be just the right height, stays in the memory, as does the illustration of him serving a hedgehog (Mrs Tiggy-Winkle, the washerwoman, no less) with a bar of soap, entering it in a notebook, bowing, and saying, 'With pleasure, Madam.'

After a while, a dormouse and his daughter began to sell peppermints and candles. When John Dormouse was complained to about candles which drooped in hot weather, he stayed in bed and said nothing but 'very snug,' which, the author tells us, is no way to run a retail business. The moral is: Don't sell faulty goods and never give tick.

My third book is Patrick Leigh Fermor's *Between the Woods and the Water*. I am sorry to say I have not read it, but I look at it every day, as it has been on the table by my bed since it was published. It comes under the dangerous category, because I know that if I am rash enough to start it, I will miss it terribly when it is finished. My journey will be the ideal opportunity to try his journey, and if I keep it till last and am still floundering about with the others when I arrive at the other end of the world, I can go on looking at it like I have for years.

Next comes *The Best of Beachcomber*, by J. B. Morton. The world has turned upside down since the column in the *Daily Express* delighted us, and now the characters, so outrageous then, are all over the place in real life. Narkover and the headmaster, Dr Smart Allick, are quite tame, as public schools go. Captain de Courcey Foulenough's bid for a seat in Parliament makes me mourn Screaming Lord Sutch,* whose slogan of 'Vote Loony—You Know It Makes Sense' was reminiscent of the captain's policy for Democracy and Duty Free Lard.

The captain was elected for South Mince and Tiddlehampton in spite of disgraceful scenes at his meetings in the headquarters of the Mince Steam Laundry Playing Fields Association. His opponent, the lovely Miss Boubou Flaring, stood as an Independent Liberal or an Independent Progressive Liberal—she could not decide which. Foulenough dismayed his supporters by changing his platform to Independent Progressive Liberal and saying 'a split vote is just as much fun as any other sort of vote.' He stood for 'work for all, friend-

---

*David Sutch (1940–1999), musician and leader of Britain's Official Monster Raving Loony Party.

ship with every nation, national reconstruction, national revival, higher wages, higher exports, higher imports, lower taxation, rearmament, peace, co-operation, co-ordination, and no closing hours.' This seems strangely familiar in 1999.

The next headline announced 'Foulenough in.'

No sooner had he taken his seat in the House of Commons than the mace was missing, which was only to be expected from one educated at Narkover under the third generation of Smart Allicks. 'Speculation ran, or rather waddled, rife as to the motives of the theft. The name of Foulenough is being freely mentioned, and it is assumed that he walked off with the symbol of British umtarara in a fit of absent-mindedness. Nobody can believe that he intended a deliberate insult to the majesty of the House, *et tout le bataclan du tralala*.'

The entertainment offered by the Filthistan Trio is a bit near the knuckle now. The three Persians, who played seesaw in the hall at the Ritz by placing a plank across the belly of the fattest, most likely own that hotel of sacred name by now, although they returned to Filthistan long ago.

You may remember the twelve red-bearded dwarfs. They plagued Mr Justice Cocklecarrot by their inane answers to his questions in the case brought by Mrs Renton against Mrs Tasker, who habitually pushed all the dwarfs into Mrs Renton's hall. As we are no

longer allowed to call a dwarf a dwarf and no doubt
we will soon be stopped from describing a beard as
red for fear of insulting its owner, it is refreshing to
read the transcript of this famous case. The political
incorrectness of Beachcomber is pure joy today.

The fifth book is *The Curse of the Wise Women*,
by Lord Dunsany. It should be required reading for all
politicians who wish to understand Ireland and the
Irish. Although it is seventy years since it was published, and the events described took place a hundred
years ago, little has changed. The infinite contradic-
tions, the unseen but deeply felt currents of conflicting
thought so apparent to the lovers of that century are
brought before the reader with a terrifying impact in
the first few pages.

Mountain and bog are described by one whose
childhood was spent drinking in the very essence of
Ireland. The author was as one with both in his un-
derstanding of that mysterious, haunted land. His description of a hunt makes me thankful that whatever
Mr Blair may decree in England, he has no power to
stop foxhunting in Ireland. He should read it. If he
has any imagination he would be caught up with, and
then overwhelmed by, the thrill of it, the sight and
sound of a pack of hounds in full cry over the empty
January land that was the west of Ireland at the turn
of the century.

The narrator was a schoolboy at Eton, spending

the Christmas holidays in his faraway home. He describes Mrs Marlin, the Wise Woman, her power as a seer, her cabin on the edge of the bog, her son, who was the author's ally and knew from his mother when the geese would come and where to find snipe on shooting expeditions over the treacherous shining bog, written with the comprehension that only an Irishman has of his fellow countrymen.

Mrs Marlin saw the destruction of her world coming with the machines of the Peat Development Company, which arrived to cut the turf. Her curses terrified the operators and all were the victims of the larger power of nature when the bog itself moved and engulfed the lot of them.

Number six is a book I could not be without. *The Oxford Book of English Verse*—not the smart, thick, heavy new edition but Arthur Quiller-Couch's 1900 anthology, reprinted in 1920 on feather-light India paper. The inscription 'Unity Mitford from Uncle G. 8 August 1925' is inside the cover—my sister's eleventh birthday.

One of the requirements of our home education was to learn a poem by heart each term. As our governesses often left and a new one came, the easiest way to do this was to choose the poem learnt the term before. Several times, I got away with this simple ruse. The poem I loved was 'The Lament of the Irish Emigrant,' by Selina Dufferin. The first lines, 'I'm sitting on the stile, Mary, / Where we sat side by side, / On a bright May morning long ago, / When first you were my bride' still brings tears to the eyes. No new edition includes these sentimental, tragic verses dedicated to a victim of the famine leaving his home and his dead wife and baby for the New World.

This leaves me with four more books to bundle into the holdall. I confess I am stumped. I might take Thomas Hardy's *The Woodlanders*, but I think it would make me unbearably homesick, so these six much-loved volumes will do. I must go back to looking out of the window or copy my friend who has done that journey and find a pack of cards for a spot of Patience to pass the time till the samovar comes round again.

Best Gardening Books

There are enough books on gardening to fill miles of shelves, and they proliferate at an alarming rate. In the October issue of *The Garden*, there is a list of 706 *new* titles on subjects as diverse as 'Vascular Plants of Minnesota' to 'Cites Cactaceae Check List' via 'Fern Names and Their Meanings' and 'A Key to

Egyptian Grasses.' Add them to those already in print and you will be totally fuddled and have years of reading ahead.

To choose a favourite from such a bewildering variety is almost impossible. I imagine that the Desert Island Discs rule, where you are not allowed the Bible or Shakespeare, applies. That eliminates the loved reference books: *The Royal Horticultural Society Dictionary*, *Trees and Shrubs Hardy in the British Isles*, by W. J. Bean, *Hilliers Manual of Trees and Shrubs*, even Graham Thomas's sixteen volumes of distilled wisdom. Having sadly put these aside, I find I like the old books best. Like old cookery books, they are quite different from those published now. They were ordinary book shape; the text was printed on thick, almost blotting, paper. There were no photographs, or a few hopelessly bad ones in black and white with a glimpse of forgotten elms beyond the garden wall. They are a pure pleasure to read.

In the last few years, we have been bombarded by the new style of gardening books. They have grown in size as well as numbers. They are too heavy to hold, so shiny that they make you blink, and the photographers (these books contain mostly photographs) can't have a decent night's rest in May and early June as they dash from Cornwall to Sutherland while the fashionable flowers are out. Striped tulips, striped roses, alchemilla, crambe, and allium must be caught in their prime. The wielder of the camera pauses just long enough to add the Kiftsgate rose, with its mates Bobbie James and Wedding Day, breaking down apple trees in the old orchard.

All very wonderful, but I would like to see these gardens in August, when the photographers have gone away.

With some famous exceptions, I don't want such books myself, but I am thankful that they exist, because very soon they are reduced to half price and sell like hotcakes in the shop at Chatsworth.

So, back to the old friends. I love *Potpourri from a Surrey Garden*, by Mrs C. W. Earle, first published in 1897. It is sprinkled with reassuring turn-of-the-century advice on bringing up children, food, and health, as well as sensible words on gardening.

In the days when they lived in the same vicarage for decades, reverend gentlemen produced some lovely books on flowers. Try *In a Gloucestershire Garden*, by the Rev. Henry N. Ellacombe, *A Prospect of Flowers*, by the Rev. Andrew Young, and, latterly, the Rev. Keble Martin's best-seller *The Concise British Flora*, a worthy successor to those two blessed volumes of my childhood by Bentham & Hooker.

These aren't gardening books, you'll say, because they are about wildflowers. But tell me of a garden today which dares not have an ever-growing plot of corn cockles, poppies, pink campion, and clover.

E. A. Bowles and his crocus; V. Sackville-West, that mistress of English who set a gardening fashion sixty years ago which is still going at full steam ahead—the list of loved ones grows. But just wait till you open *The Anatomy of Dessert*, by Edward Bunyard (1929). Let him describe the minute difference between varieties of peaches, the very week at which they are at the zenith of deliciousness, the way a melon should be handled, and the smell of a perfect fig.

In doing so, he conjures up the dream garden, its greenhouses, hotbeds, heated walls, fruit cage, nuttery, and, of course, the sublime head gardener, who produces these marvels to the minute for the delight of the owner and his guests.

There is no question of anything so vulgar as selling the delectable produce to people who might not appreciate their finer points. Mr Bunyard could not have left home for so much as a day between May and October, or he would have missed the prime moment of one or another of his fruits.

Sometimes he is lyrical. In the chapter on pears, he writes, 'Happy those who were present when Doyenne de Comice first gave up its luscious juice to man. Here at last was the ideal realised, that perfect combination of flavour, aroma and texture of which man had long dreamed.' And so he describes all the fruits grown in this country, denigrating or eulogising according to his taste.

A more matter-of-fact help for amateurs and professionals alike is *The Small Garden*, by Brigadier C. E. Lucas Philips. How I wish I had met this man whose handsome face is on the last page of my paperback of 1962, now nicely browning at the edges.

He is at his best when describing the downside of his subject. Pest number one, he says, is the jobbing gardener. If he had lived till now, I wonder if he would have said it is the strimmer.

The chapter called 'The Enemy in Detail' and the treatment thereof is so funny and so well written, it carries you along like a thriller. What other gardening writer would describe cuckoo spit thus: 'Inside a mass of frothy spittle is a curious soft creature which, on disturbance, will attempt to escape by weak hops'? The brigadier tells you all you need to know. Seek no further and send the rest of your books to the jumble.

Now for *the* favourite—about a kitchen garden, which I prefer to lawns and flower beds.

It is *The Tale of Peter Rabbit*, by Beatrix Potter. Held in the palm of the hand, the luxury of wasted space on the pages, the razor-sharp narrative, the warning by the hero's mother not to go into the neighbouring garden because his father was put in a pie there by the gardener's wife—all make you long to see what the place was like. You must read several pages before you arrive there, with mounting anticipation. How much better than being begged to visit with opening hours and price of admission attached. I'm sure Mr McGregor would never have allowed people in and would have attacked the British public with his rake or any other weapon close at hand.

Beatrix Potter is not only my favourite author; she is my favourite artist. The illustrations have the magic quality of leaving a lot to the imagination. You are allowed only a corner of the cucumber frame, a couple of pots of chrysanths (no flowers on them, luckily), some meagre cabbages, a gooseberry bush, a little pond, one robin, and three sparrows. But you can picture the whole through the Westmoreland mist.

The gooseberries, whose net impedes the escaping rabbit, are not Leveller or any such shiny and tasteless invention. They are red and hairy, Bunyard's 'ambulent fruit,' good enough to please the master himself.

The two classic edgings to the vegetable beds are beautifully drawn: stone for a stone country, and box, which looks right everywhere.

I confess that nostalgia plays a part in my love for this book. Mr McGregor's dibber, a wooden wheelbarrow, a real besum, real flowerpots, and a proper tin watering can are balm to the eyes of this old-age pensioner. A proper gate, too, made on the place and not bought from a garden centre.

Peter feasts on lettuces, French beans, and radishes till he feels sick. He goes in search of parsley to settle his stomach and comes across a pond. He can't (but we can) enjoy its construction of this Lake District stone, no concrete to be seen, and the water lilies and flag iris which grow in it. The trouble is a white cat studying the goldfish, whose tail 'twitches as if it were alive.' She is as much of a threat to a rabbit as Mr McGregor himself. The relief when our hero just manages to escape after so many hazards is enormous.

But it is the image of that northern garden which has stayed in my mind's eye all my life, and it is without doubt my favourite.

FOURTEEN FRIENDS
by James Lees-Milne

James Lees-Milne was looking for a title for his latest book. We were discussing it and one of my granddaughters asked what it was about. 'Fourteen friends,' I said, 'all dead.' Without hesitation, she said, '*Stale*

Mates.' An excellent title, I thought, before I read it. Dead the mates may be, but stale they are not. Brought to life as the author knew them, they are described in his inimitable way. He remembers an absurd or sad detail which stays in the mind and nails some facet of the personality of his subject to a tee.

I was interested to know about the hardships of John Fowler's* early life, of which I knew nothing. I often wondered whom his face reminded me of, and J.L.-M. has it with Tenniel's Duchess in *Alice in Wonderland*. Latterly, he tells us, courage was necessary on the part of the client to ask John to work on a house. Courage was needed to be his servitor. I carried his patterns for him when we were doing up a house belonging to the National Trust. He sent me scurrying up and down the Long Gallery at Sudbury, drawing curtains to get a certain light, undrawing them, pinning bits of stuff here and there, and moving furniture at his command. It was no good crying for mercy. He would have given a pitying look at such frailty when, already mortally ill, his whole being was focused on the job at hand. But when we got home in the evening, his barked-out orders were forgotten and we

*John Fowler (1906–1977) was the most influential interior decorator in the traditional style in the 1950s and 1960s, and a partner in Colefax and Fowler with Virginia-born Nancy Lancaster.

laughed till bedtime. J.L.-M.'s portrait of John describes him perfectly and is one of the best in the book.

Kathleen Kennet* discovered that J.L.-M. had been asked by *The Times* to write her obituary. She bombarded him with letters full of details about her achievements, even pursuing him by post to Italy to keep him up to the mark, lest he should leave out a plum or two. It would have been easier if she had written her own obituary, like distinguished people write their entries in *Who's Who*. I am quite glad that K.K. is one of the mates I did not know. Yet J.L.-M. loved her.

Vita Sackville-West is another matter. She was the inventor of a style of gardening which is still mimicked all over the world, a poet and an original, but seeing her craggy face and shapeless form in the photograph we know so well, it is impossible to believe that she inspired such passion as is described. But we must believe it, because no one was immune. Men and women alike fell under her spell. Her husband referred to her affairs as her 'muddles.' So muddled am I by the variety of her conquests that I long for explanations. Why did she have to 'masquerade as a

*Kathleen Kennet, sculptor. Married: 1. Capt. R. F. Scott, the Antarctic explorer; 2. Edward Hilton Young, the first Lord Kennet.

wounded Tommy in the streets of London' to delight Violet Trefusis? At a charity concert where Vita recited, Lady Crewe, the organiser, announced that 'she would pass the Queen round to the left like port.' J.L.-M. 'remained a faithful fan' and exhorts us to do likewise. I just wish I had met this heady mixture of Clark Gable and Marlene Dietrich with 'eyes of glowing coal' and an exceptionally beautiful voice.

The description of Henry Yorke/Green* makes me wonder why J.L.-M. took so much trouble over him, and wonder even more how people could have enjoyed his dreary novels, the quotes from which are dispiriting in the extreme. He states that Henry had 'very beautiful manners.' This sentence might have been left out had he been a fellow guest when the Yorkes stayed with us in Ireland many years ago. Henry sat in a heap for a week and did not speak except to say, when gazing out of the window at the rain, how much he hated the country. His wife was indeed saintly to look after this morose man until he died.

Two who were changed beyond all recognition as time slipped away were James Pope-Hennessy† and Everard Radcliffe. The former was beautiful, funny,

---

*Henry Yorke, novelist, who wrote under the pseudonym Henry Green.
†James Pope-Hennessy was a writer; he was murdered in 1974.

and clever, with intuitive charm, and was an inspired writer. His friendship with J.L.-M. had its ups and downs, and some of the downs must have been hard to forgive, but 'his merriment was infectious, his charm insidious.' On a National Trust jaunt to Suffolk, he says to the author, 'Being with you is like being with myself, only nicer.' No wonder Jim rejoiced in such company. Alas, drugs, drink, and 'mad larking' turned Jamesey into a near demon who met a grisly end. J.L.-M.'s last glimpse of his beloved companion of better times, from the top of a bus in Trafalgar Square, makes the blood run cold.

Radcliffe inherited Rudding Park, near Harrogate. He was as much in love with the place as Vita had been with Knole and devoted his life to the well-being of its estate and to adding works of art to embellish the house and garden. When money troubles caught up with his extravagances, he played a protracted game of cat and mouse with the National Trust over his inheritance. On the point of signing, and without a word to the Trust, Everard put the place on the market and decamped to Switzerland, leaving the love of his life to become the inevitable conference centre. His story is nearly as sad as poor Jamesey's.

Fourteen Friends is compulsive reading. The author's generosity of spirit shines through the descriptions of the disparate characters we come to know. He notes the faults as well as the virtues of his mates, but he does not criticise, and loves them in spite of all. Lucky people.

James Lees-Milne. *Fourteen Friends.*
London: John Murray, 1996.

A MINGLED MEASURE
by James Lees-Milne

Everyone who enjoyed the other 'Kubla Khan' diaries will fasten with joy on to this volume, which covers the years 1953–1971. J.L.-M. was no longer working full-time for the National Trust, so there are no more hilarious descriptions of meetings with owners of houses considered for handing over. But it is a wonderful picture of the life of this observant man, who describes places, artists, writers, neighbours, friends, and relations and allows us in on some of his own thoughts.

Forty years on, some people seem as extinct as dodoes—Eddie Marsh,* for instance, who criticised so

---

*Sir Edward Marsh (1872–1953): Private secretary to Winston Churchill (1917–1922 and again 1924–1929) and also private secretary to the Duke of Devonshire (1922–1924).

sharply a manuscript of J.L.-M.'s that it made the author miserable for days; a rag-and-bone man uttering his cries in Thurloe Square; and Hilaire Belloc setting himself on fire by his candle while staying with a friend. J.L.-M. arrived at Nice airport at 3:40 a.m. and walked the six miles to Alvilde's (his wife since 1951) house in Roquebrune. The installation of electric light at Westwood Manor in Wiltshire is noted and deplored. These are memories of a long-lost world.

The Lees-Milnes lived at Roquebrune for ten years, she passport- and tax-bound, he going to and from his flat in Thurloe Square. They hobnobbed with the locals, from Prince Rainier to the curé's cousin (her mother kept a tame hen, whose tail feathers trimmed the frame of her photo—the hen's, I mean, not the mother's), the Graham Sutherlands, the local goatherd, and annual visitors to the coast, including Winston and Clementine Churchill. There lived a witch in the village, and Somerset Maugham down the road. When a mistral blew up, spreading sparks, which caused a disastrous fire, over their garden of little ledges and up the steep hillside to the very walls of their house, I didn't mind as much as I should have done.

In 1964, the Lees-Milnes moved to Alderley Grange in Gloucestershire. 'The perfect mid-Georgian house,' wrote Candida Lycett-Green. 'Inside a grand and generous staircase rose from a pale stone-flagged hall patterned with black stone diamonds.' Here, Alvilde's twin accomplishments of cooking and gardening were appreciated by all who had the luck to taste or see the results of her work. In spite of frequent visits to London for the opera (where they always seemed to land in the royal box), plays, exhibitions, and some committees of the National Trust which still bound him to that organisation, one feels that the diarist was really at home in that magic part of the country.

He walked in the woods with his whippets, and in spite of saying he always looked at his feet, he noticed everything. The more he noticed and loved what he saw, the more gloomy he became over what was happening to England. He often found himself among friends who bewailed the state of the country, politically and aesthetically. His favourite places were threatened by motorways or drowning in a reservoir—even a new cowshed filled him with gloom. Watching the 1972 Trade Union Congress on the television convinced him that 'communism must come to this country within 25 years.' I do hope he is comforted by the fact that there are only three years to go and it somehow doesn't seem likely. The same year, Denys Sutton* 'thinks an immediate revolution possi-

*Art critic and editor of *Apollo*.

ble and an authoritarian government absolutely essential. George Weidenfeld* said exactly the same thing a
week ago.' Well, well.

Later that month, Caroline Somerset† took the
Weidenfelds round Badminton and Lady W. said to
C., 'Did it take a long time to find such a beautiful
house?' I expect that was several Lady Weidenfelds
ago.

A friend who had been to Chequers told J.L.-M.
that Mr Heath, unable to bear sleeping in the room
which had been Mr Wilson's, chose another. That is
the most human thing I have ever heard about Mr
Heath.

'Went last night to the Handley-Read collection of
Victoriana at the Diploma Gallery. The hideousness
and stuffiness of the furniture and ornaments beyond
belief—sheer lodging house, and no wonder both
Handley-Reads committed suicide last year.'

I've never heard of the Handley-Reads or their
horrid collection, but the aesthete in J.L.-M. was not
surprised by their grisly end after one glance at what
the poor things had accumulated.

*British publisher.
†Lady Caroline Thynne (1928–1995) in 1950 married David Somerset, later eleventh Duke of Beaufort.

People who have grown up since the years of the
war and immediately after can have little idea of what
this country owes to J.L.-M. He rescued, almost
single-handedly, scores of delectable buildings, each
one unique. It was before the word 'heritage' was
chucked around to justify keeping everything from a
badger sett to a banjo. No one bothered then. Pull
them down; leave them to rot; these buildings will
never be needed again—that was the attitude of those
in command. Had it not been for his dogged persist-
ence against all the odds, including public opinion, local government opinion, and up, up to the cabinet
itself, none of which had the slightest interest in things
of beauty and legislated accordingly, the poor old heritage would have been a great deal poorer. J.L.-M. is
far too modest to underline any of his achievements,
but he is lauded by everyone who remembers them.

In my ignorance, I could have done with some
guidance here and there. Who was Father Illtud Evans,
whose death saddened (only momentarily, I admit)
J.L.-M.? Why did Monica Baldwin want help? I long
to know more about Bertie Towers, who bought ancestors to go with a manor house and of whom 'Alec
Clifton Taylor had little opinion.'

There are a number of spelling mistakes, wrong
dates, and asterisks the second time a person is mentioned, and some places don't appear in the index—

unworthy of the house of John Murray and surely not the fault of the writer. Never mind. I read it with intense pleasure because *A Mingled Measure* brings J.L.-M. into the room, and who could be a better companion on an autumn evening?

James Lees-Milne. *A Mingled Measure*.
London: John Murray, 1994.

DEAR MARY
by Mary Killen

What trouble people get themselves in, what mix-ups and muddles, and not only in 'social life,' where the chilling word 'etiquette' still appears to rule. (I thought it had gone with the war: wrong, as usual.) Every hour of every day, the most worrying things seem to happen.

Many of them arise from the inhibited British being unable to face unpleasantness head-on. It would be much easier to say to an offender, 'You smell,' or 'Please stop eating in such a disgusting way,' but we have been brought up not to do that. Instead, we ask Mary Killen, and she knows just how to smooth the way, whatever the problem.

I have great sympathy with some of her correspondents—the unlucky S.M. of Wiltshire, for instance, who sat next to the Foreign Secretary at dinner, didn't recognise him, asked what he did, failed to hear the word 'Foreign,' and spent the rest of dinner discussing shorthand typing. Too late to ask for advice, I am afraid.

E.S. of W11 has joined a health club in Notting Hill and lives in terror of seeing Antonia Fraser bare. You must buy the book to see the inspired answer to this one.

Since beloved David Cecil died, I am no longer troubled by the problem of C.S. of Islington, who asks, 'What is the correct way of removing spittle which someone has accidentally spat onto one's face while talking enthusiastically?' So I didn't bother to read the answer.

I pity poor A.M. of Fonthill, whose wife is addicted to telephoning faraway friends before the cheap time. If my father had caught me doing that, his reaction would have been to hand out the short, sharp shock treatment which a Home Secretary advocated for certain offences a few years ago. I don't suppose nice Mary would ever suggest anything so drastic, but I heartily recommend it to A.M.

L.G. of Ludgershall asks how to stop her weekend guests from stealing books. I'm afraid that is a dreadfully difficult question, especially as they always bag the most readable. Mary's solution, copied from the late Lord Moyne, tells L.G. to have a supply of stiff cards and make the borrower write his name, address, and date of borrowing and put it in the space in the shelf where the book was. A good plan, but not as threatening as that of my sister when she was married to the same Lord Moyne. Their bookplates read 'This book was stolen from Bryan and Diana Guinness.'

The perennial agony of forgetting names is the subject of two letters. D.L. of SW1 suffers from it, and as he/she works in publishing and, I presume, has to attend such ghoulish entertainments as book launches, he/she will be delighted with Mary's clever solution. But what struck me about his/her letter was not the problem but the fact that he/she states, 'Flattery and ego-stroking are integral parts of my job.' How I should love to meet this individual, surely the rarest of birds in that profession where bosses and employees all seem to lack the most basic good manners (always excepting the late Jock Murray).

The best thing about being old is having grown out of minding most of the social pitfalls described in these letters. In years gone by, I was as vulnerable as the next person, and one frightful evening stands out. I found myself sitting at dinner next to M. Pompidou, then President of France. He spoke no English, I no

French. Our host sat opposite us across a narrow table, greatly amused by our predicament. We sat there crumbling bread and trying to smile at each other. Dear Mary, where were you that evening?

Mary Killen. *Dear Mary: The* Spectator *Book of Solutions.* London: HarperCollins, 1993.

I ONCE MET
edited by Richard Ingrams

The Oldie's *I Once Met* is a game of Consequences full of unexpected twists and turns. If only the famous had known they were being met by someone who was going to describe the encounter years later, they would surely have behaved differently.

One exception, I guess, is Field Marshal Viscount Montgomery of Alamein, who still would have barked out a ticking-off to the unlucky boy from Westminster Abbey Choir School in whom he was interested. In 1953, he more or less ordered the boys to take photographs of him and his page standing in a nearby doorway, dressed to the nines for the coronation. David Ransom was one of them. The next day, the *Daily Mail* carried a photograph of the scene.

In the foreground stood young David, bent over his box Brownie camera. Alas, one of his socks had collapsed round an ankle. Such sloppiness was too much for the old soldier, and the next day the poor fellow was summoned to the headmaster's study to face Monty himself, who reprimanded him in military fashion.

Many meetings with famous actors and actresses are described. In my experience, such encounters are nearly always disappointing. It is better to watch them plying their trade than to meet them face-to-face. Selwyn Powell saw a brilliantly funny performance by Harpo Marx in a variety show at the Palace Theatre. He followed him back to the Savoy to photograph him for *Picture Post*—but not one word does Mr Powell remember of what the great comedian said. (Now I come to think of it, wasn't Harpo the one who couldn't speak?)

When A. N. Wilson was twelve, he called on L. S. Lowry to seek advice on painting. The house in Salford was coal black outside and chaotic inside. The artist, 'his white hair en brosse like a polar bear's,' told the boy he preferred the Sunderland seaside because he couldn't paint trees. Twelve-year-old boys don't know when to leave, so after hours of his unplanned company, Lowry said he would see A.N. back to Manchester and deliver him to his mother, who was having tea at Marshall & Snelgrove. In this case, it would have been interesting for the roles to have been reversed, so we could know what L.S. thought of A.N., who didn't dare go back for the portfolio of paintings he had left behind.

Oscar Hammerstein cured Donald Sutherland's stomach ulcers by a prescription of a soluble capsule and a packet of Dreft washing powder taken daily 'for a while.'

John Mortimer met Robert Graves on a sofa (I told you it was Consequences). Graves said to Mortimer, 'Jesus Christ, of course, lived to the age of 80, when he went to China and discovered spaghetti.' Jo Grimond, also on the sofa, asked, 'In which gospel do we read that Jesus Christ went to China and discovered spaghetti?' 'It's not in a gospel. It's a well known fact of history,' answered the poet.

Vincent Brome, an ardent admirer, interviewed the dying H. G. Wells. Wells let loose a diatribe against God, the monarchy, Parliament, and Bernard Shaw. Women, whom Brome imagined Wells had been rather fond of, were a necessary encumbrance to the life of a man. Humanity itself was dismissed as 'a parcel of sweeps.' Brome left, disillusioned.

The Last Squire of Erdigg was a natural for the series. When Mr and Mrs Michael Strachan went to see the house newly opened to the public, they found the

Squire struggling with a clockwork spit from which hung a stuffed pheasant. He asked where they were from. 'Scotland,' they said. 'So you know David Baird?' They did. On the strength of this unlikely exchange, the Strachans suggested taking him out for dinner. A series of disasters with boarded-up restaurants followed, ending with the hospitable Squire asking them to stay the night in his nearby cottage. His last guest had been a tinker: 'Splendid fellow, but needed a bath.' So did the purple sheets in the spare room, and the Strachans were thoroughly flea-bitten.

Sir Alec Guinness, Fangio, Lord Wavell, Matisse, Graham Greene, Hitler, Sir Jack Hobbs, Richard Widmar, and Sir Matt Busby all come out of it rather well. Philip Larkin, Ronnie Kray, and E. M. Forster don't. Neither does Randolph Churchill.

More Cartoons, also edited by Richard Ingrams, and *The Oldie Dictionary of Our Time*, edited by Mike Barfield, were included for review with *I Once Met*. Alas, I don't understand either of them, in spite of trying quite hard. But I do understand and can thoroughly recommend *I Once Met*.

I Once Met. Edited by Richard Ingrams.
London: Oldie Publications, 1996.

THE NATIONAL TRUST MANUAL
OF HOUSEKEEPING
by Sheila Stainton and Hermione Sandwith

Not since Mrs Beeton's *Household Management* of
1861 and its many updated editions has such a complete guide to housekeeping (or house-*maiding*, rather,
as surely house*keeping* includes food and the kitchen)
been available to those who have charge of what are
now called historic houses. Through this absorbing
book, the housemaid herself is turned into the next
best thing to a museum curator.

After forty-one years at the job, I am shaken by the
number of things which can go wrong. I am conscious
of sins of omission which spell disaster. The mysteries
of how or, more importantly, how not to treat the objects in your care are explained in fine detail, and we
learn the latest methods of conservation and the professional care of all manner of things. The way to
clean rooms from cellars to attics, and the infinite variety of their contents, from model ships to ancient
textiles, big-game trophies to marble floors, are described. The methods set out are by perfectionists for
perfectionists. No shortcuts, no sweeping the dust under the carpet. The dire consequences of slacking are a
purple warning to all who care for 'things.'

The book is aimed at houses which are 'put to

bed'—that is, dust-sheeted from top to bottom—for the winter. Houses which are lived in often have their busiest time round Christmas, so some of the rules do not apply to them.

The houses were built, decorated, and furnished at the behest of their owners and meant to be lived in. The owners had families, which meant children, dogs, canaries, white mice, and other pests which discomfited the starched housekeepers of yesteryear. Yet the houses survived with a surprising number of artefacts intact. The deeper you get into the book, the more amazed you are that there is anything left at all, and the guiltier you feel about actually using a room or its furniture.

Hide-and-seek, sardines, kick the can, catapults, roller-skating down passages, billiard fives, and other pastimes of successive generations of children belonging to the house would drive the authors of this book mad. What would they make of the sixth Duke of Devonshire ('the Bachelor Duke,' 1790–1858) writing of his childhood at Hardwick Hall? He wrote, 'I turned the recess [of the dining room], in which the billiard table now stands, into a kind of menagerie: a fishing net nailed up under the curtain confined the rabbits, hedgehogs, squirrels, guinea-pigs and white mice that were the joy of my life from 8–12 years old. The smell caused by these quadrupeds and their vegetable diet

was overpowering; but I would have been very surprised had any objection been made to their residence
here.'

The gallant housemaids worked away through the
rough-and-tumble of family life, turning huge mat-
tresses daily, and carrying hot water to distant bedrooms. They served a long and stern apprenticeship,
which taught them much of what we learn from this
book.

The hazards of keeping the simplest things in order
appear to be overwhelming. If it is too difficult, consult an expert.

We know that light is the enemy (Granny used to
say that moonlight was even more destructive than
sunlight) and blinds must be kept down. We must
beware of 'dust and airborne pollution, fluctuation
of temperature and humidity, attack by moth and
worm.' If the rooms get too dry, my instinct is to open
the windows—but in flies the carpet beetle. Having
made a meal of the spirea in the garden, he turns his
attention to the Axminsters. Birds also fly in, so you
must put a net over the windows. In this house, they
choose the best pictures on which to make messes.
Thinking of messes, I looked up 'dog' in the index for
advice on the inevitable where they are concerned, but
could find only 'dog-eared.'

And what about the infamous bacon beetle? I bet

you didn't know that this little epicure, denied the food after which he is named because there is no breakfast in National Trust houses, likes nothing better than to gorge himself on a globule of fat from the belly of your best stuffed fish.

If the rooms are too damp, surely the answer is to light the fire. But if you have steel grates, you must engage a metal conservator to put them right in the morning. That would be expensive at Chatsworth, as he would be a daily visitor in the winter.

Outdoor shoes are banned. Dustproof mats do their job perfectly, but the way your shoes stick to them gives you the terrifying sensation of being unable to run away from a pursuer in a bad dream.

Disease is rife among inanimate objects. There is a bronze disease and a pewter disease, mother-of-pearl gets Bryne's disease, and ink attacks the paper on which it is written. Minerals are not always healthy. The diseased stones at Chatsworth so enthralled my sister Nancy that she described their malady in one of her books, *The Pursuit of Love*.

We have come a long way since Granny went round Hardwick with a little mallet, banging the furniture to give concussion to the woodworm.

I greatly admire the National Trust for setting such standards. I know they carry them out, because I have seen them at it. It is going to be a job to live up to them. After reading this book, I am going to try to be acid-free myself, to eschew the company of exuberant children and animals, and generally look to my house-keeping.

There is a mine of information here, and the list of suppliers of equipment and materials and their addresses is an invaluable work of reference in itself. I shall look after my copy with proper care.

Sheila Stainton and Hermione Sandwith. *The National Trust Manual of Housekeeping.* London: Penguin, 1991.

HOW TO RUN A STATELY HOME
by John, Duke of Bedford, and George Mikes

All Russells are clever and original, and the thirteenth Duke of Bedford is no exception. His lovely little book, *How to Run a Stately Home*, has been re-published in paperback fourteen years after it first appeared. It will give immense pleasure to all in the trade and to the millions of people who support it.

Let us remind ourselves why the Duke threw himself into the stately business with such gusto, shocking his peers, who disapproved of the publicity he sought and so readily found.

In 1953, his father died unexpectedly, and he found himself the owner of Woburn Abbey: house, works of art, garden, park, farms, woods, and the rest that attaches itself to such a place; and there was a bill for the regulation £5 million death duties. Lesser men would have taken the advice of the family solicitor, sold up, and fled to Monte Carlo: not the Duke of Bedford. Immediately, he began to feel the irresistible pull of the Territorial Imperative.

Reading a book on monkeys, he realised why he was determined to hang on to it. 'It all started with the monkeys who each insisted on having his own special private place up in the trees of the primordial forests. We humans have inherited this healthy and natural instinct from our ancestors: We must each have our own place. This territorial imperative is, basically and ultimately, the impulse that makes me go on fighting. I want my own place. This place happens to be it and I am determined to keep it. I am the owner . . . of a magnificent Stately Home; I am also the monkey on the tree.' He set about making Woburn the most famous and visited house in England, and in no time, he succeeded.

The Duke had owned the place for eight years when he wrote the book, and much experience had been gained. By then, he felt qualified to tell the others how to do it, and in the nicest possible way he has done so. It is remarkable how his fiercest critics have come to heel.

His advice to ditherers who could not decide whether to open their houses was 'go ahead,' and they all have. *But first build your lavatories.* They all have. A friend of mine who is a distinguished architect tells me that his most usual commission by far is for lavatories. The Duke goes on to the tearoom, the complement of lavatories (or have I put the cart before the horse, as it were?). These two are the prime necessity for a successful Stately. Then comes the essential shop.

After you have given thought and energy to, as well as having spent a great deal of money on, this holy trinity, you must pay attention to the hangers-on: the house, garden, and park. However, having got the first three right, the latter will fall into place beautifully.

Why do people come? the Duke asks himself. Because they have got a car and they must drive it somewhere. They can spend a day in the English equivalent of Disneyland, a world of make-believe, of Rembrandts and Sèvres, state rooms and tapestries which have nothing to do with reality. No one can imagine putting a baby to bed or knitting in front of the fire in such rooms, and so they are transported to the unfamiliar plane of someone else's rarefied life. In an hour

or two, the visitor can be back in the womblike secu-
rity of his own car. He has seen wonderful things; he
is glad to have seen them, but the last thing he wants
is the responsibility of owning them.

That may be true, but what brought the crowds to
Woburn was the benign and friendly presence of the
Duke himself, exuding his fondness for the human
race, always on hand to chat, to sign, and to sell. He
was Exhibit A in wonderful surroundings.

After fourteen years, the language seems a little
old-fashioned. Stately Homes have become Historic
Houses. Their owners are no longer people like the
Duke of Bedford, but trustees, who, for some unknown reason, always come from London. Lavatories
were Toilets for years; now they are Facilities and
are apt to sprout bossy notices like NOW WASH
YOUR HANDS. Tea is still tea, as far as I know,
but the part of the estate which is open is a Unit, a
Scene, or a Complex. Souvenirs are Gifts now, except on Sundays, when they must revert to being
Souvenirs to satisfy the Alice in Wonderland trading
laws.

The word 'heritage' appears only once in this
book, and then in its proper context. Environment,
conservation, vandals, and leisure are not mentioned
at all. Good.

And so we learn How To Do It. Having done it,

the Duke left the Stately scene as he had arrived. Grandson of the Flying Duchess,* son of the twelfth Duke, whose best friend was a spider,† he is much missed as the undisputed innovator in the little world of Houses And Castles Open To The Public.

John, Duke of Bedford, and George Mikes. *How to Run a Stately Home*. London: André Deutsch, 1985.

Stolen Books

I suppose our friends are as honest as the next lot, but it is odd how books disappear. Not the fat and heavy biographies of politicians in two volumes, which no one could read in bed (or out of it), but the attractive ones you pick up over a weekend and don't have time to finish. They vanish like summer snow, and although I sometimes search every room in our huge house, I never find the missing loved one. So I have resorted to selfishness, gathering irreplaceable volumes in my room, where it is unlikely that anyone would

*Mary, the eleventh Duchess of Bedford (d. 1937), famed for her penchant for aeroplanes.
†John, the thirteenth Duke of Bedford, mentioned this in his autobiography.

bag one, even from the pile on the floor. Perhaps my unstealables would not appeal to everyone. *Fowls and Geese and How to Keep Them* (1935, one shilling sixpence, and worth every penny); *Book*, by Lady Clodagh Anson, and *Another Book*, by the same author—classic descriptions of Anglo-Irish life before the Great War; nice, thin 1930s Betjemans, *Continual Dew* and *Mount Zion*; the real *Oxford Book of English Verse* on India paper, the poems chosen by that professor whose name is a mixture of duvet and sofa, Sir Arthur Quiller-Couch; *What Shall We Have Today?*, by X. Marcel Boulestin (what did X. stand for?); and *The Life of Ronald Knox*, given to me by good, kind Evelyn Waugh, who knew I can hardly read, so, mercifully, the pages have no words on them. They are all blank. A book which would disappear by next Monday if left in a visitor's room is *A Late Beginner*, Priscilla Napier's autobiography. Brought up in Egypt and seeing pyramids against the sunset from her nursery window, she asked, 'What are they, Nanny?' 'Tombs, dear. Where's your other sock?' You can't do better than that, and I do not want to lose it. The works of George Ewart Evans are next to *The Secret Orchard of Roger Ackerley*, by Diana Petre; *White Mischief*; *The Prince, the Showgirl and Me*; *The Day of Reckoning*; *Rio Grande's Last Race*; and books with pages covered in print, dash it, by E. Waugh,

P. Leigh Fermor, and J. Lees-Milne. Most precious is *The Last Train to Memphis: The Rise of Elvis Presley.* If that goes, I give up.

Patrick Leigh Fermor at Eighty-Five

Paddy Leigh Fermor, eighty-five? Not possible! Yet I am told he was born in 1915 and that it is his birthday today. Hardly a grey hair, upright, trudging for miles up and down dale or swimming for hours, according to whether he is in England or Greece, he is adored by my youngest grandchild as well as by his own generation: an ageless, timeless hero to us all.

I first saw him nearly fifty years ago at a fancy dress party in London. He was a Roman gladiator armed with a net and trident, and his getup suited him very well. I had heard of him, of course. Everyone had. By 1957, the story of his exploits in occupied Crete had been made into the film *Ill Met by Moonlight*, with Dirk Bogarde as Paddy. It is still shown on telly from time to time.

It was in 1942 and 1943, living so closely to them in shared danger, that he became deeply devoted to the Cretans, and the bond between him and his old comrades is as strong as ever.

Paddy and his great friend Xan Fielding* had lived in the Cretan mountains, disguised as shepherds (I wouldn't put him in charge of my sheep, but never mind), for eighteen months, in constant danger of being caught by the enemy, before the spectacular coup in 1944, when he and Billy Moss, an officer in the Coldstream Guards, kidnapped the German commander, General Kreiper, which earned him the DSO. Their prize was bundled into the back of the German official car while Billy Moss drove them through a town in the blackout, Paddy sitting on the front seat, wearing the general's cap in case anyone should glance at the occupants. After a four-hour climb on foot to the comparative safety of a remote cave in the mountains, they spent eighteen days together, going from one hiding place to another and sharing the only blanket during the freezing nights. When the sun rose on the first morning and lit up the snow on the summit of Mount Ida, the general gazed at the scene and quoted a verse of an ode by Horace. His captor completed the next six stanzas. Such a duet under such circumstances must be unique in the history of war.

When he was sixteen and a half, he was sacked from King's School Canterbury for holding hands with the greengrocer's daughter, sitting on a crate of

*Xan Fielding (1918–1991): Heroic wartime secret agent and author.

veg. What to do next? A military crammer was tried but didn't seem to suit, so he mooned around London, making friends who lasted a lifetime. At the age of eighteen ('and three-quarters,' he says for accuracy), he yearned to go to Greece. He could not afford the fare, so he walked there. What a lesson to young people now who write to strangers asking for money to enable them to travel. Years later, his walk inspired *A Time of Gifts* and *Between the Woods and the Water*, perhaps the two most acclaimed of all his books, winners of endless literary prizes and translated into more languages than probably even Paddy knows. His love of Greece prompted him and Joan to build their glorious house on the sea at Kardamyli, living in a tent and working with the masons till it grew into the idyllic place where they live now.

He is one of those rare birds who is exactly the same with whomever he is talking to. Children recognise him as a kindred spirit. With his formidable scholarship and prodigious memory, he is just as able to spout Edward Lear or 'There was an old woman as I've heard tell, who went to market her eggs for to sell' for them as Marvell or Shakespeare via Noël Coward for grown-ups.

I have got stacks of letters from him. They usually begin 'In Tearing Haste' or 'In Unbelievable Haste,' and the writing jolly well shows it. This one is dated

1956, when I evidently had omitted to ask him to give a hand at my funeral: 'Your lovely letter was marred by this business about pall bearers. You tell me all about enlisting John and Xan with never a hint of asking, when I am exactly the right height, own a dark suit and a measured tread and would really look sad.' Forty-four years on, this is a bit near the knuckle.

He wrote me a hilarious account of a disastrous visit to Somerset 'not Willy to me, alas' Maugham at the Villa Mauresque. He was taken there by Ann Fleming. All went well the first day, but soon he got deep in the mire by imitating someone who stammered. As this was an affliction of Maugham's and one about which he was extremely sensitive, it was too much for his host, 'who offered a limp handshake and said "Well [I won't indicate the stutter, too late, alas!] I'll say goodnight and goodbye too, as I'll still be in bed when you leave.' Worse was to come. 'I had a new case with a zip and when I zipped it up the beautiful Irish linen sheet with WSM embroidered on it caught and was torn with a rending noise from top to bottom. There was nothing for it but to do a bunk.' He was cheered to learn 'that Cyril [Connolly] had once been made to leave the Villa Mauresque for picking and eating the last avocado on the single tree.'

These sort of letters make me look forward to the post.

Try and get him to sing 'It's a Long Way to Tipperary' in Hindustani and his translations in Italian of 'John Peel' and 'Widdecombe Fair.' John Peel's hounds—Ruby, Ranter, Ringwood, and True—turn into Rubin, Vantardo, Rondo Bosco, Campinelli, and Fidele.

'Tom Pierce, Tom Pierce, lend me your grey mare / All along, down along, out along lea' becomes '*Tommaso Pierce, Tommaso Pierce, prestami tua grigia giumenta / Tutti lungo, fuori lungo, giu lungo prato.*'

And Cobley's gang are 'Gugliemo Brewer, Giacopo Stewer, Pietro Gurney, Pietro Davey, Daniele Whiddon and Enrico 'awke. *Ed il vechio zio Tommaso Cobley e tutti quanti,*' et cetera.

Or the longest palindrome, 'Live dirt up a side track carted is a putrid evil,' delivered, for some unknown reason, in the broadest Gloucestershire accent. Just the entertainment for a winter's night.

Andrew regards him as a latter-day Byron and thinks it fitting that Byron and Paddy share the same publisher. Handsome, funny, energetic, and original, he is a brilliant, shining star—how lucky my family and I are to have had such a friend for so long. Happy birthday, Paddy!

Being Painted by Annigoni and Lucian Freud

 We had seen some portraits which Annigoni had done, and Andrew decided to commission him to paint me. I had to go to his studio in London every day for a month. We couldn't talk to each other, since he spoke little English, and I no Italian. The telephone often rang, and I would answer it for him; it was usually a girlfriend.

There was no discussion about how I would pose; he was the master and he would decide. He almost always painted an imaginary landscape in the background with a fisherman, which was a sort of signature. I got the distinct impression that painting me was just a chore for him; he was not enjoying it much.

Lucian Freud's picture of me, painted four or five years later, was a different matter. Lucian is an old friend and a charming, generous man (at least to his friends). I think I was the third member of our family whom he painted. I went to his studio for three hours every morning when I was in London, over several months. I can still remember the strong smell of paint in his studio. He works very slowly, often starting from one eye. Sometimes, when I arrived, he would say, 'I had a wonderful night. I removed everything I did yesterday.' (He often works at night.) People often say that I look so sad or bored in the painting. I defy anyone not to look a bit wooden after sitting for so long.

There were interruptions, with bailiffs calling. Lucian is a huge gambler, and his fortunes seemed to change all the time. Sometimes, because he had pawned his car, I lent him mine, and once when I arrived for a sitting, he held out my car keys and said, 'This is all that's left'—the car had been stolen.

I'm not sure that I can judge the success of pictures of myself. I think my head is a little too big in the Annigoni, and perhaps his is more of a pretty picture; whereas Lucian captures the essence of people. Freud doesn't like anyone to see a painting before it is finished. Eventually, we were allowed to look. When Andrew arrived at the studio, someone else was already there. Andrew looked long at the picture, until the other man asked, 'Who is that?' 'It's my wife.' 'Well, thank God it's not mine.'

Road from the Isles

In the 1930s, my parents bought a small island off the coast of Mull. Called Inchkenneth, it lies about a mile out to sea from the tiny village of Gribun: To the west, there is no land till you reach America. It is a romantic and beautiful place and in fine weather has a serenity found only in such places which are difficult of access and empty of human beings.

The weather was all-important; there was much tapping of the glass and listening to every BBC forecast, as the narrow channel between the island and Mull became very rough with little warning, and we were often cut off for days at a time. For this reason, the island had to be self-supporting in the necessities of life, and could produce some luxuries as well. There was a walled kitchen garden which had been there when Dr Johnson stayed on the island in his tour of the Hebrides in the eighteenth century. Oats, hay, and potatoes were grown on the small enclosed field, and we had lobster pots and trawled for mackerel, and at spring tides there were even oysters and mussels for the picking. We kept chickens and ducks, so there was no shortage of eggs. Sheep and bullocks completed the farm stock and grazed the unenclosed hill.

There were three house cows. To have a continual supply of milk was the aim, of course, but the problem of calving at a certain date, never easy, was made acute by the fact that each cow had to swim to Gribun to visit the bull. Cows can swim well when they have to. There was a large sloping rock which she was led across, and the tide had to be just right so that, with a mighty heave, she could be pushed into the water without too much fuss. The boat at once set off, towing the cow by a rope around her horns. All too often, it started to blow a gale when this vital journey was to take place—and so another three weeks would go by until we could try again.

The result of such curiously vague mating arrangements was that one summer, when the house was full of visitors and children, all the cows were dry and there was nothing but tinned milk, which no one liked. So my mother decided to buy a goat. She found a British Saanen of uncertain ancestry and gave it to me. She was called Narny, and a more charming animal you could not imagine: everyone liked her from the beginning. She was free to go where she liked, and she used to jump onto the retaining wall of a steep bank by the kitchen door to be milked—fresher milk there never was.

My mother soon added more goats to the farm stock and had some beautiful British Saanens, large and quiet, and wonderful milk producers. It was an ideal place for them, as they had the run of the island, a mile long, and were able to graze on ledges and places where even the sheep did not dare go. They had bells round their necks, and the whole effect was beautiful when they were grazing on the stretches of grass and salty herbs which ran down to the sea.

I was on Inchkenneth when war was declared in September 1939, and I had to go back to Oxfordshire. Naturally, I could not leave my goat behind, so, together with a whippet and a Labrador, we set out on a journey which, at that time, took twenty-four hours.

We left the island at 6:30 a.m., in the dark. At low tide, there was a long walk over seaweed-covered rocks, and it was impossible to reach the boat without stepping into a pool or slipping over. Wet, and often grazed as well, we undertook another hazardous walk over the rocks on the coast of Mull to the tin hut where the car was kept. Sometimes that car was agonisingly stubborn about starting. There was no other means of transport, and it was eleven miles across Mull to Salen, where the mail boat called only once a day to go to Oban, so one could be stuck for twenty-four hours if the car did not co-operate. The goat travelled in the rickety old luggage trailer, covered by a tarpaulin against the driving rain.

The mail boat was well equipped for such passengers as my animals. At that time, it was the only transport for all farm stock as well as humans; one could safely give anything from a bull to a book of stamps to the staff, and either would be miraculously delivered to the right person at the other end.

The boat took three hours to get to Oban, with two stops on the way, through some of the most beautiful scenery in Scotland. There was a long day to pass in Oban, as the London train did not leave till the evening. After a few weeks on the island, it was always exciting to see shops again, and the goat and the dogs dutifully followed round. A greengrocer and a butcher provided their meals for the day.

It was dark again when the time came to go to the station at the other end of the harbour. Goat in the guard's van, dogs in the carriage, we settled down to one of those endless wartime journeys with a dim light and crowded train.

In the middle of the night, we arrived at Stirling, where we had to change and wait an hour for the London train. I milked the goat in the first-class waiting room, which I should not have done, as I only had a third-class ticket. Luckily, no one noticed. The dogs were delighted with their unexpected midnight drink of new milk, and, relieved and refreshed, we boarded the London train.

There was a long queue for taxis at Euston, and I was rather apprehensive that when my turn came, the driver might not be too willing to take on such a curious assortment of passengers; but, luckily, he turned out to be one of those cheerful Cockneys who are not put out by anything, and the four of us arrived at my sister Nancy's house in perfect order—just ninepence extra on the clock. She lived in Blomfield Road and had quite a big garden, so Narny feasted on Nancy's roses. Enough pruning was done in two hours to last for a long time—as all goat and garden owners will understand.

Paddington Station was within walking distance, but the hurrying London crowds did not notice the dishevelled party of girl, goat, and dogs.

Narny lived for a long time, produced twins every year and an enormous amount of milk, but I shall always remember her for her perfect behaviour on the journey from the Hebrides to Kingham.

Childhood

My childhood seems to belong to another world. Some thought our upbringing strange, even then, but we didn't—children just accept what they find.

I was born in 1920, in my parents' house in London, the youngest of a family of seven, six girls and one boy. My eldest sister, Nancy Mitford, was sixteen when I was born—then came Pam, Diana, Tom, Unity, and Jessica.

My mother's dearest wish was to have a big family

of boys, and every time another girl was born, there was bitter disappointment.

Nancy used to tell me with glee of the gloom that descended on the house when they heard of my birth.

Until I was six, we lived in an Elizabethan manor house called Asthall in the beautiful Cotswold valley of the Windrush. A few years ago, when the house was for sale, the agent took my husband and me to see round it. I had been in it only once since we had left to live at Swinbrook, seventy-two years before. It was a strange feeling to see the empty rooms and to remember how many people had lived there from 1919 to 1926—seven of us children, Nanny, a nursery maid, a governess for the older ones, Mabel and her helper in the pantry, Annie the head housemaid and two young girls under her, Cook and a kitchen maid, an odd man, Mr Dyer, and my father and mother. In this company, our lives were secure and regular as clockwork. We had parents who were always there, and an adored Nanny, who came when Diana was three months old and stayed for forty years.

'The barn,' converted by my father and separate from the main house, was a haven for Nancy, Pam, Tom, and Diana. They had the run of my grandfather's excellent library—Nancy and Diana always said it gave them their interest in literature. Music was my brother's passion, and his piano was in this big room.

Our nursery looked out over the churchyard, and we younger ones were forbidden to watch funerals, which of course made them more fascinating, and we always did. Jessica and I once fell into a newly dug grave, to the delight of Nancy, who pronounced that we should have bad luck for the rest of our lives.

Our animals were as important to us as were the humans in the house—mice, guinea pigs, a piebald rat belonging to Unity, poultry, and goats. The big animals of farm and stables, the garden, which seemed so huge to a small child, the village beyond the churchyard, the post office, where acid drops were one and a half pence a quarter in a twist of paper, weighed on the same brass weighing scale as the letters—that was our world. We knew no other.

In the summer, we bathed in the river and in winter, we skated on the flooded frozen fields between Widford and Burford.

Nancy wrote a lot about our childhood, of course, in *The Pursuit of Love* and *Love in a Cold Climate*, which, to her amazement, became best-sellers, and people still ask me, 'Was your father really like Uncle Matthew in the books?'

He was, in lots of ways. He could get terrifyingly angry, and we were certainly in awe of him, but at the same time he was wonderfully funny and the source of all the jokes in the family. He and Nancy together were better than anything I've ever seen on the stage.

The fact that one couldn't always judge his mood made things exciting, and we all played the game of Tom Tiddler's Ground to see how far we dared go before he turned and bellowed at us.

He hunted my older sisters with his bloodhounds, which surprised the neighbours. He was punctual to the second. If he expected someone at one o'clock, he would start looking at his watch at six minutes to and with a furious face say, 'In seven minutes, the damn feller will be late.'

In London, he did all his shopping at the Army and Navy stores and used to be there well before the doors opened at nine. When my mother asked why he had to arrive so early, he said if he left it any later, he was impeded by 'inconveniently shaped' women.

My father was no good at business and always seemed to be on the losing side of whatever he went into. He was one of the first in the great gold rush in Canada in the 1920s, but the acres he staked out were the only ones for miles where there was no gold.

Because of this land and other similar ventures, plus the Depression of the thirties, we lived in smaller and smaller houses. I was thankful when I grew up that there was no longer room for parties of young people to come and stay, as I had observed from the safety of the nursery how terrifying it could be for the unsuspecting young men friends of my sisters.

My father did not exactly make them feel at home. If there was a pause in the conversation at meals, he used to shout down the table to my mother, 'Have these people no homes of their own?'

One friend was banished into the snow because he bent down to pick something up for my father and a comb fell out of his pocket. A man, carrying a comb . . . He was the nineteen-year-old James Lees-Milne, the distinguished writer, who remained friends with us all to the end of his life, in spite of this strange treatment.

My parents hated social life and we seldom saw any-one but the family, local uncles, aunts, and cousins, and one another. I never remember them going out to meals, nor hardly ever having anyone to our house until my sisters grew up. I suppose my mother was taken up with everyday life and so many children, but my father used to go to London to attend the House of Lords, where he was chairman of the Drains Com-mittee.* He came back with rich tales of his fellow peers, who were even odder than they are now. At

*No doubt it had a grander name, but drainage was the subject de-bated.

home, he saw to the farms and woods and the multi-farious jobs to do with an estate.

Being the youngest, and sometimes the favourite of my father, I soon learnt that tears nearly always succeeded in getting me what I wanted and getting the others into trouble for teasing me.

In other ways, though, being the youngest wasn't so good. I never had any new clothes, always the wretched cut-down things of the sisters. Pocket money was less, just because of being younger. My sister Unity, called 'Bobo,' had far more than even her age warranted, because my mother said she *liked* money more than the rest of us. This led to a shouted chorus, which was used about everything. 'IT IS UNFAIR; Bobo's got a rat and lots of money and I haven't got anything.'

'IT IS UNFAIR' was the great cry. But as everything in life is unfair, perhaps the sooner it is realised, the better.

My mother had unusual views on health. We were brought up on the Jewish laws about the subject—no doubt very wise in the climate of Israel before refrigerators, but hardly necessary in Oxfordshire. We could have only meat which 'divided the hoof and chewed the cud' and fish which had 'tails and fins'; therefore, no pig meat and no shellfish were allowed.

My father, of course, had what he liked, and we used to long for the sausages which he had for breakfast and the cold ham covered in burnt sugar which appeared on shooting days. Once in a while, Mabel used to risk all and let us finish what came out of the dining room, and we danced round the pantry with a delicious end of congealing sausage.

My mother didn't believe in doctors. Her theory was that if everything was left alone, the 'good body' would right itself. If we were very ill, a masseuse used to appear. We were the envy of our friends, in that we not only weren't forced but were not allowed medicines or, the panacea of all childish ills, syrup of figs or, worse still, castor oil.

She wasn't in the least interested in whether or not we had been to the lavatory. She knew it would happen sooner or later, and if it was later, well, never mind. The 'good body' would work in the end.

And we were never made to eat food we didn't want. This was rare in those days, and I am always thankful for it. I think it is a refined cruelty to force children to eat what they don't like or to finish something they don't want.

Our own curious ideas of food were usually given in to, if rather unwillingly. Bobo lived on little else but mashed potatoes for two years, and I had a passion for bread sauce, which I had with every meal, and Bovril spread on bread and butter. My mother tried to put me off this by saying it was made of old horses' hooves. I suppose it was the equivalent of children nowadays liking only chips and ice cream.

When Jessica had acute appendicitis, my mother conceded that her appendix must come out. The operation was done on the nursery table. No one thought it in the least bit odd, having it done at home. We were all a bit jealous of the fuss made of her, and there was a great deal of 'IT IS UNFAIR' when the appendix was given to her in a jar full of that stuff that preserves such things.

My mother was before her time in many of her theories. We always had bread made at home out of whole-meal flour. But we longed for and continually asked for 'shop bread,' though we hardly ever got it.

She and my uncles regularly wrote to the papers on what they called 'Murdered Food'—refined white sugar, white flour from which the wheat germ had been removed, and so much else which is fashionable now, seventy years on. They were considered to be eccentric then.

An instance of her contempt for the scientific was the time tuberculin testing for cows came in when I was about eleven. We had Guernsey cows, and the butter, milk, and cream they produced were wonderfully good. My mother was told that three cows had reacted to the test. 'Which are they?' she asked. As always in such cases, they were the three best-looking in the herd. 'What, get rid of those lovely animals? Certainly not! The children can have their milk.'

And had it we did, with no ill effects of any kind, which served to underline her distrust of scientists and doctors.

We didn't go to school. My father didn't approve of education for girls. My brother, yes, he went through the conventional programme without question, but the girls, no. My father didn't mind us learning to read and write, perhaps because my mother taught us till we were seven, but the idea of anything more annoyed him very much indeed.

My mother didn't agree. She hadn't any money of her own, so she started a chicken farm. Only the cracked and soft-shelled eggs came into the house, and my sisters said that the only chickens we had to eat were those which had died. From the small but regular profit, my mother paid for a governess—so, to the schoolroom we had to go. I don't know if there were school inspectors in those days. If so, would they have got past my father?

I am sorry to say that there was not just one governess but a succession of the unfortunate women. We were perfectly foul to them and made their lives intolerable, so, naturally, they left. My sisters had been through a fair few of them before I came on the scene. And we may have been awful to them, but some of them were pretty peculiar, too.

Miss Pratt only liked playing cards, so we played

Racing Demon from 9:00 till 10:30, half an hour break, then again till lunch. We became very good indeed at it.

Miss Dell encouraged us in the difficult art of shoplifting—well, stealing really.

None of us ever went in for an exam of any kind. We were spared the torment that children suffer now, and I certainly would not have passed any of them.

 My best friend during all these years was our old groom, Hooper. Every moment that I was not forced to be doing something else was spent in or around the stables. We understood each other completely, which I suppose was just as well, as he had a terrific temper (which, I discovered years after, was due to some terrible experiences and shell shock suffered in the Great War).

I believe people now would think my parents were taking a bit of a risk, allowing a child of ten or so to spend so much time with such an erratic fellow. When Bobo did something which annoyed him, he'd say, 'I'll take yer in that wood and DO for yer.'

But he never did.

To me, he was the human end of the horses and ponies I so adored, and the stables were my heaven, as were the woods and the little roads, many of them still untarred, of the few miles roundabout, which in the days before horse boxes were our boundary.

We went to church, of course. My father used to take the collection and tortured us by stopping twice at my aunt and giving her a nudge the second time. She would frown at him and slap his hand, which started us on the peculiar agony of church giggles.

My sisters were all very strong characters and totally different from one another, yet, like all families, we still had a strong link, which survived grown-up differences of politics. We were an awful family for nicknames, and all seven children had constantly changing names for one another.

Nancy was a tease on the grand scale, and because she was so much older and so much cleverer, we younger ones used to believe her. Nothing was ever dull when she was around.

We were once set a question by my mother of how we would budget if we were to live away from home on a set amount of money—three hundred pounds a year, I think it was. We all broke it down most carefully, so much for rent, so much for rates, heat, light, food, and clothes. Nancy finished ages before the rest of us. She had just put down 'Flowers £299, Everything Else £1.'

Her success as a writer was born first of all from her wonderfully accurate observations of my father and our family life, and when she graduated from novels to historical books, their success was due to sheer hard work. Totally uneducated, she applied herself with complete dedication to her subject and set it down as only she could.

The next sister, Pam, was as different from Nancy as you could imagine. Immersed in country life, her animals, her garden, and, above all, her kitchen—she was a wonderful cook—she was the Martha of the family.

My brother, Tom, was the third child, adored by both parents and all sisters, hardly known to me, as he always seemed to be away at school. Lawyer, musician, and soldier, he was killed in Burma at the very end of the war. My parents never recovered from this tragedy.

Diana came fourth, the cleverest of the family and beautiful to look at at all ages.

Then Unity, funny and loyal and brave, bigger than life-size in every way. She died when she was thirty-four.

Jessica was the sixth, the curly-haired favourite of Nanny, and my beloved companion and ally against the others when persecuted. She lived in America and fought fiercely for the cause of the underdog. Like Nancy, she has a certain reputation as a writer. When she was little, she dreamed of a completely different life from that in which she was brought up. Pocket money and Christmas windfalls from uncles all went into her Running Away Fund. Her sights were set on a bed-sitting room in the East End of London.

A most determined character, she did indeed run away, in 1936, and when we discovered she had gone to fight for the Communists in Spain, all Nanny said was 'But she didn't take any clothes to fight in.'

Nanny was a wonder, really a saint. I never saw her cross or heard her say an unkind word to anyone, and highly tried she must have been. At the same time, she didn't mete out any praise, and sat on any signs of vanity which my sisters might have been forgiven for having.

'Oh Nanny, I can't go to the party in this AWFUL dress.'

'It's all right, darling. No one's going to look at *you*.'

This dictum was carried a bit far when Diana, eighteen years old and staggeringly beautiful in her wedding dress, said, 'Oh, Nanny, this hook and eye doesn't work. It will look awful.'

'It's all right, darling. Who's going to look at *you*?'

The only holidays we ever had (it was the days before everyone had to go away for holidays) were with Nanny's sister, whose husband had a hardware shop in the main street of Hastings. The wonderful smell of paraffin and polish, the beautiful brushes hanging down from the ceiling, and the freezing-cold grey sea, with a ginger biscuit as reward for going in—it was all lovely in its way, but as we couldn't take ponies, goats, rats, mice, guinea pigs, and dogs, it seemed a waste of a fortnight to me.

I look back on my childhood as a very happy time. It is unfashionable to do so, I know, but the idea of school, so longed for by my sisters, was anathema to me. Spared that horror, I was conventionally and boringly happy, I suppose, and thought our upbringing was like everyone else's.

But, on looking back, I don't think it was.